ST. ANSELM'S

BOOK OF

MEDITATIONS

AND PRAYERS

Contents

Contents

INTRODUCTION

THE See of Canterbury, in a period of hardly more than one hundred years, was held by three of the greatest Saints of England--St. Anselm, St. Thomas, and St. Edmund. These three, wonderful in their perfection, each distinct from the other, and in the gifts which constituted that perfection, had all one task, which was to vindicate the liberty and purity of the Church by suffering, by exile, and, though only one received the martyr's crown, by the sacrifice of a martyr's will. Yet how variously the Holy Ghost ripened and formed them! St. Anselm's chief perfection was the illumination of the speculative intellect by the gifts of science and understanding: that of St. Thomas the elevation and grandeur of the will by fortitude and holy fear: that of St. Edmund the sanctification of the practical intellect by the gifts of counsel and of wisdom.

The works of St. Anselm exhibit an intellectual light, order, subtilty, penetration, and precision which give him a high place among the scholastic theologians of whom he was the forerunner and the guide. But even in the purest intellectual exercise of the reason, his writings are pervaded by the gift of piety, which makes its, warmth sensibly felt. He may be regarded as the type of faith, rendering to God the reasonable service of the intellect. This rationabile obsequium, which is the highest perfection of the human intelligence, springs from faith. Reason precedes faith indeed in judging of the motives of credibility: and the last act of reason judging of evidence precedes the first act of faith in believing the revelation of God. But when revelation has been once received, the grace of faith is unfolded by the gift of intellect into the faith which is one of the twelve fruits of the Holy Ghost. Faith as a virtue illuminates the intelligence, but faith as a fruit of the Holy Ghost understands, so far as God permits, the intrinsic reason of what it believes. St. Anselm explains his whole method in these words: As the right order demands that we should first believe the deep things of the Christian faith before we venture to discuss them by reasoning, so it appears to me to be negligence, if, after we are confirmed in faith, we should not endeavour to understand what we believe.' [1] Here we have his method in direct contradiction to the rationalism of these later days, which makes reason the test, the measure, and the criterion of faith, destroying thereby the essence of faith, as well as the matter proposed to its belief. As St. Augustine says, If you ask of me, or of any other Doctor, not unreasonably, that you may understand what you believe, correct your definition, not so as to reject faith, but so as to perceive by the light of reason the things which by the firmness of faith you already hold. . . . Therefore it was reasonably said by the Prophet, "Unless you believe, you will not understand,"' [2] so St. Anselm begin where he prefers. And, indeed, it is for this reason that they have been divided into sections; [3] that the reader may easily choose a place for beginning or for stopping, and so avoid the weariness and annoyance which would be produced by too prolonged application to the book, or by repeated reperusal of one and the same passage; and that he may thus be the more likely to reap some pious dispositions from them; for this was the end had in view in their composition.

[1] Cur Deus Homo, lib. i. c. 2.

[2] De peccat. merites, c. xxi. 16, tom. x. p. 16.

[3] [Ad hoc enim ipsum paragraphis sunt distinctæ;' divided into sections by means of marks in the margin; or, divided into sections by means of inserted headings. Thus in one of his letters (i. 20), writing of some prayers to the Mother of God composed by him, he says, Denique idcirco volui eas ipsas orationes per sententias paragraphis distinguere, ut anticipando longitudinis fastidium, ubi volueris, possis eas legendo incidere.' Of the meditations attributed to St. Anselm, the majority, as we find them in the printed editions, are not characterised by bracketed headings or by subtitles; nor are their obvious subdivisions indicated by what we should call unbroken paragraphs. The translator has therefore ventured to insert into such of the meditations as do not in the printed editions show where they are capable of an unforced subdivision, a suitable subtitle, or at least a numerical indication. He has done this not irreverently, he trusts, to the saint, nor impertinently, he ventures to hope, to the reader. To the compassion of the one and to the indulgence of the other does he commit himself; adding only this, that whatever has been inserted by him is included within square brackets.]

FIRST MEDITATION

OF THE DIGNITY AND THE WOE OF MAN'S ESTATE.

[§1.] I. Our creation to the Image and Likeness of God. Awake, my soul, awake; bestir thy energies, arouse thy apprehension; banish the sluggishness of thy deadly sloth, and take to thee solicitude for thy salvation. Be the rambling of unprofitable fancies put to flight; let indolence retire, and diligence be retained. Apply thyself to sacred studies, and fix thy thoughts on the blessings that are of God. Leave temporal things be hind, and make for the eternal.

What, then, in so divine an occupation of the mind, canst thou conceive more useful or more salutary than to recall in delighted musing thy Creator's boundless benefits to thee? Consider what grandeur and what dignity He bestowed on thee in the very beginning of thy creation, and ponder well what loving and what adoring worship thou shouldest therefore pay Him.

It was assuredly a noble purpose which He formed for the dignity of thy state, when, creating and ordering the universal frame of the visible and the invisible creation, He determined to make man; for He determined to lavish richer honours on man's nature than on all other creations in the universe. Behold thy lofty origin, and bethink thee of the due of love thou owest thy Creator. Let Us make man,' said God, to Our Image and Likeness' (Gen. i. 26.). If thou awakest not at this word, O my soul; if thou art not all aflame with love of Him for His so ineffable graciousness of condescension towards thee; if thine inmost marrow burns not with longings after Him, what shall I say? Asleep shall I call thee? Or must I rather think thee dead? Consider diligently, therefore, what it is to have been created to God's Image and God's Likeness; thou hast in this thought the sweet earnest of a pious meditation in which thy musings may have full play.

Observe, then, that likeness is one thing; image another. For example, the horse, the ox, or other dumb animal may have a certain likeness to man; but the image of man is borne by none but a human being. Man eats, so does the horse; here is a certain likeness, a certain something common to creatures of diverse moulds. But the image of man is only borne by some human being, some being of selfsame na-

- 7 -

ture with that man whose image he is. Image, therefore, is of a higher order than likeness.

God's Likeness, then, may be attained by us in this way; if, musing on Him as the Good, we study to be good; if, owning Him the Just, we strive to be just; if, contemplating Him the Merciful, we make endeavours after mercy.

But how to His Image? Listen. God ever remembers Himself, understands Himself, loves Himself. If thou, therefore, after thy poor fashion, art unweariedly mindful of God, if thou understandest God, if thou lovest God, thou wilt then be man to His Image;' for thou wilt be striving to do that which God does eternally. 'Tis the duty of man to bend his whole being to this task; the task of remembering, of understanding, and of loving the Highest Good. To this idea should every thought and every turn and folding of thy heart be moulded, chased, and formed; to be mindful of God, to understand Him, and to love Him; and thus savingly exhibit and display the dignity of thine origin in that thou wast created to the Image of God.

But why say that thou wast created to His Image, when, as the Apostle testifies, thou art in deed His Image? The man,' he says, ought not to cover his head, because he is the image and glory of God' (1 Cor. xii. 7).

[§ 2.] II. To praise God eternally the end of our creation. Are, then, these so incalculable benefits of thy Creator inducements enough to thee for continual thanksgiving in return, and for discharging the debt of an endless love; when thou considerest that out of nothing--rather, out of clay--thou wast raised by His bounty to so excellent a dignity in the very beginning of thy state? Test thy life, therefore, by the master-feeling of the saints, and note well what is said of the saint, With his whole heart he praised the Lord' (Ecclus. xlvii. 10). Behold the end of thy creation, behold the task set thee as God's servant! Why should God have graced thee with the privilege of so illustrious a lot, if He had not willed thee to apply thyself unceasingly to the praise of Himself? Thou wast created for the glory of thy Creator, that, making His praises thy employment, thou mightest ever advance towards Him by the merit of justice in this life, and mightest live happily in the world to come. For the praise of Him yields the fruit of justice here, and of beatitude hereafter.

And if thou praise Him, praise Him with all thy heart, praise Him by loving; for this rule of praising has been laid down for the saints--With all his heart he praised the Lord, and loved God who made him' (ib.).

Praise then, and praise with all thy heart; and whom thou praisest, love; for, for this wast thou created, to praise Him, and to love Him also. For that man praises God, but not with all his heart, who is charmed by prosperity into blessing God, but checked by adversity from the privilege of blessing; whilst that man praises, but without loving, who amid his praises of God seeks for some other good in praising than God Himself. Praise therefore, and praise aright; in such wise that there be in thee no care, no aim, no thought, no anxious bent of mind, uninspired by praise of God, grace helping thee. From praise of Him let no prosperity of this present life seduce thee, nor no adversity restrain thee; for thus shalt thou praise Him with all thy heart. But when thou shalt praise Him with all thy heart, and praise with the homage of thy love as well, then wilt thou desire nothing from Him but Himself, and thou wilt pray that the object of thy longing may be God; the reward of thy toil, God; thy solace in this life of shadows, God; thy possession in that blissful life to come, God.

Yes, indeed, thou wast created for this; to praise Him, and to praise Him without end; which thou wilt then more fully understand when, entranced by the blessed vision of Himself, thou shalt see that by His sole and gratuitous goodness thou, when thou wast not, wast created out of nothing; so blessed, and to such unspeakable bliss created; created, called, justified, glorified. Such a contemplation as that will give thee an untiring love of praising Him without end; from whom, and through whom, and in whom thou wilt rejoice in being blessed with blessings so great and so unchangeable.

[§ 3.] III. Wherever we are, we live, move, and are in Him; whilst also we have Him within us. But, returning from the beatitude that is to be, do thou with the eye of contemplation consider for a while the abundance of grace wherewith He hath enriched thee even in this fleeting life. He, very God, whose dwelling is in heaven, whose throne among the angels, He to whom heaven and earth, with all that they contain, do bow down and obey, has offered Himself to thee as thine abode, and furnished and prepared His presence for thee; for, as the Apostle teaches, in Him we live, and move, and be' (Acts xvii. 28).

9

So to live, how sweet! So to move, how lovable! So to be, how desirable! For what more sweet than to have life in Him who is the very life of bliss itself? What more lovable than to rule each movement of will or act of ours towards Him and in Him, seeing that He will stablish us in an unending security? What more desirable than in aspiration and in act evermore in Him to be, in whom alone--or rather who alone--is true being, and apart from whom none can rightly be? I AM WHO AM,' He says (Exod. iii. 14); and beautifully said it is, for He alone truly IS, whose Being is unchangeable. He, therefore, whose so unapproached Being is being in so transcendent and unique a sense that He alone truly IS; in comparison of whom all being is no being; when He would create thee to so great excellency that thou couldest not even comprehend the lustre of thy dignity, what did He set as the sphere of thy being, what place of abode did He furnish for thee? Hear Him Himself speaking to His own in the Gospel, Abide in Me, and I in you' (St. John xv. 4). O inconceivable condescension! O blissful abiding! O glorious interchange! What condescension of the Creator, to will that His creature should in Him have dwelling! What inconceivable blessedness of the creature, to dwell in the Creator! How great glory of a rational creation to be, by so blessed an interchange, associated with the Creator, as that He in it and it in Him should have their dwelling! Yes, He of His mercy has willed that we, so highly ennobled in our creation, should have the farther dignity of dwelling in Him. He, governor of all things, without care or solicitude existing over all; He, source and foundation of all things, without toil sustaining all; He, superexcellent above all things, without vain-glory transcending all; He, embracing each and every thing that is, without extension of Himself enfolding all; He, the plenitude of all things, without narrowing of Himself, fulfilling all,--yes, indeed, He, though His Presence is nowhere wanting, has chosen for Himself a kingdom of delights within us; the Gospel bearing witness where it says, The Kingdom of God is within you' (St. Luke xvii. 21). And if the kingdom of God is within us, and if God dwells in His realm, does not He whose kingdom is within us abide Himself within us? Clearly so; for, in like manner, if God is wisdom, and if the soul of the just is the dwelling of wisdom, he who is truly just has God abiding in him. And the Apostle says, The temple of God is holy, which temple you are' (1 Cor. iii. 17).

Do thou, therefore, apply thyself unweariedly to the pursuit of holiness, lest thou cease to be the temple of God. He Himself says of His own, I will dwell in them and walk in them' (2 Cor. vi. 16). Doubt not, therefore, that wherever there are holy souls, there He is in them. For if thou art in those limbs of thine which thou quickenest, wholly and in all their parts, how much more is God, who created thee and thy body, wholly present in thee through and through? It is thy duty, then, to think with most intense devotion with what considera- tion and what reverence we should control those senses and those members of our body, over which the very Godhead sits in charge. Let us offer, therefore, as is meet, the whole empire of our heart to so great an Indweller, that nothing in us may rebel against Him; but that all our thoughts, all the movements of our will, all our words, and the whole course and tenour of our actions may wait upon His beck, stand obedi- ent to His will, and be conformed to His rule of right. For thus shall we truly be His kingdom, and He will abide in us; and we, abiding in Him, shall live aright.

[§ 4.] IV. All of us who have been baptized in Christ have put on Christ. Rouse thyself, my soul; rouse thyself, and let the fire of a love from heaven blaze in thy inmost parts, and learn thou carefully the dignity bestowed on thee by thy Lord God; and learning, love; and loving, revere with the addresses of a holy practice. Does not He who has assigned thee a dwelling in Himself, and has deigned to dwell in thee, does not He clothe thee, deck thee, and adorn thee with Himself? As many of you,' says the Apostle, as have been baptized in Christ have put on Christ' (Gal. iii. 27). What worthy meed of praise, then, and of thanks wilt thou pay Him who has invested thee with such grace and exalted thee to so great dignity, as that with thy heart's hap- piest outburst of joy thou mayest well exclaim, He hath clothed me with the garments of salvation, and with the robe of justice He hath covered me' (Is. lxi. 10)? To the angels of God, to gaze on Christ is supremest joy; and, lo, of His infinite condescension He has bent Him- self to thee so low as to will thee to be clothed with Himself. What sort of clothing can it be, but that of which the Apostle glories when he says, Christ . . . is made unto us of God wisdom and justice and sancti- fication' (1 Cor. i. 30)? And with what stately robes could He have more richly decked thee than with the amice of wisdom, the apparel of justice, the fair covering of sanctification?

[§ 5.] V. We are the Body of Christ. Yet why should I say that Christ has clothed thee with Himself, when He has joined thee to Himself so intimately as to choose that in the unity of the Church thou shouldest be of His very Flesh? Listen to the Apostle as he sets forth

11

the witness of Scripture, They two shall be in one flesh; I speak in Christ and in the Church' (Eph. v. 32). And then again meditate on the closeness of union of their espousal. Ye are,' he says, the Body of Christ, and members of member.' Treat, then, thy body and its members with the respect which be seems them; lest if thou treat them wrongfully by any heedless management soever, thou be subjected to so much the severer punishment for thy unworthy usage, as thou wouldest have been crowned with a nobler prize for treating them as they deserved. Thine eyes are the eyes of Christ; therefore thou mayest not turn thine eyes to gaze on any kind of vanity; for Christ is the Truth, to whom all vanity is entirely opposed. Thy mouth is the mouth of Christ; therefore thou mayest not--I speak not of detractions, nor of lies--thou mayest not open for idle speeches that mouth which should be reserved only for the praises of God and the edification of thy neighbour.

So, too, must thou think of the other members of Christ intrusted to thy keeping.

[§ 6.] VI. In Christ we are one, and are with Him one Christ. But look deeper still, and see in how close fellowship thou art joined with Him. Hear the Lord Himself entreating the Father for His own: I will,' He says, that as I and Thou are One, so they also may be One in Us (St. John xvii. 21). I am Thy Son by nature; let them by grace be Thy sons and My brethren.' How high a privilege is this, that a Christian, mere man as he is, should in Christ be so advanced as to be in a certain sense himself called Christ! A truth apprehended by that faithful dispenser of the ecclesiastical household, who said, All we Christians are in Christ one Christ.' And no wonder; since He is the Head, we the Body; and He Bridegroom at once and Bride; Bridegroom in Himself and Bride in holy souls whom He has joined to Himself by the bond of a deathless love. As a Bride groom He hath set a mitre on My Head, and adorned Me as a Bride with ornaments' (Is. lxi. 10).

Here, then, my soul, consider well His benefits to thee; burn thou from devotion to Him; glow with flames of desire for the blessed vision of Himself; call aloud, touched with the burning ardours of an inmost love; and, melted into longings after Him, break forth into the cry of the faithful spouse, Let Him kiss me with the kisses of His Mouth (Cant. i. 1). Away from my soul, all delight out side of Him; let no attachment, let no solace of the present life allure me, so long as His blissful presence is denied me. Let Him embrace me with the arms of His charity; let Him kiss me with His mouth of heavenly sweetness; let Him speak to me with that speech ineffable wherewith He displays His secret wonders to the angels.' Let this be the interchange of addresses between the Bridegroom and the bride; I opening my heart to Him, He unfolding His hidden sweetness to me. O my soul, quickened by musings such as these, and inspired with the touch of a holy longing, strive thou to follow the Bridegroom; and say to Him, Draw me; we will run after Thee to the sweet odour of Thy ointments' (Cant. i. 3). So say, and say it faithfully, not with a quickly-fleeting sound of words, but with desires that can never flag. So speak as to be heard; so desire to be drawn to Him as to be able to follow on.

Say, therefore, to thy Redeemer and thy Saviour, Draw me after Thee. Let not the world's charms entice me, but the sweetness of Thine own most blessed love allure me. Time was I was drawn by my own vanity; but now let Thy truth draw me, draw me after Thee. Draw me, for Thou hast drawn; keep me, for Thou hast laid hold of me. Thou didst draw me to redeem, draw me to save. Thou didst draw me in Thy pity, draw me to Thy bliss. Thou didst lay hold of me, appearing among us made Man for us; keep me, keep me, now that Thou rulest over heaven exalted above the angels. It is Thy word, Thy promise. Thou hast promised, saying: And I, if I be lifted up from the earth, will draw all things to Myself' (St. John xii. 32). Draw me now, therefore, Thou so mightily exalted, even as Thou hast allured me, so compassionately humbled. Thou hast ascended on high, let me see it; Thou reignest over all things, let me know it. Do I not know, then, that Thou reignest? Yes, yes, I do, and I thank Thee that I do. But let me know by perfect love what I know by pious thought of Thee; let me know by sight what I know by faith. Bind to Thyself the desires of my heart with the links of an indissoluble love, for with Thee are the spring and source of my life. Let loving unity associate whom redeeming love has linked together. For Thou hast loved me, Thou hast given Thyself for me. Let my desires be ever in heaven with Thee; let Thy protection be ever upon earth with me. Help this heart, this heart all but breaking with desire of Thy love, as Thou didst choose it, when it despised Thy love. Give to me now that I ask; for when I knew Thee not Thou gavest me Thyself. I return, O take me home; for when I was a runaway Thou didst call me back. Let me give love, that I may have love; nay, rather, because I am loved, let me love Thee more and more, that I may all the more be loved by Thee. Let my heart's will be one with Thine; let my one sole aim be all with Thee; for with Thee our nature, assumed by Thee in mercy, now reigns glorified. Let me cling to Thee inseparably, and adore Thee unweariedly, and serve Thee perseveringly, and seek Thee faithfully, and find Thee happily, and possess Thee eternally.' Plying thy God with words like these, O my soul, take fire, and burn, and break forth in flames, and long to be all ablaze with yearnings after Him.

[§ 7.] VII. A consideration of our sins, for the which our conscience does the more sting us, and by which we have forfeited all these blessings. But whilst thou considerest to what and how great blessings thou hast been advanced by His grace, reflect also what and how great blessings thou hast by thine own fault foregone, and into what evils thou hast fallen, overburdened by a load of sins. Ponder with sighs over the ills thou hast wantonly committed; reflect with groans and tears over the blessings which by those same ills thou hast miserably lost. For what good has not thy all-bountiful Creator of His goodness lavished on thee? And what ill hast thou not paid Him in requital, grown wanton in execrable impiety? Thou hast cast away good, and merited evil; nay, made shipwreck of good, and freely chosen evil; and, the grace of thy Creator being thus lost, or rather thrown away, thou hast miserably incurred His wrath. Thou hast no resource for proving thyself innocent when a crowd of evils done by thee surrounds thee like a countless army, here confronting thee with thy unholy deeds, there marshalling an innumerable host of unuseful and, what is more to be condemned, of harmful words; and there yet again parading an infinite array of wicked thoughts. These, then, are the price for which thou hast foregone inestimable blessings; for these hast thou forfeited the grace of thy Creator. Conjure them up, and grieve over them; grieve over them, and renounce them; renounce them, and condemn them; condemn them, and change thy life to a better course. Wrestle with thyself in thy heart of hearts, lest even for a moment's space thou give consent to any kind of vanity, whether in heart, or tongue, or, worst of all, in act. Let there be a daily, or rather an unceasing, struggle in thy heart, lest thou keep any kind of covenant with thy faults. Ever and unremittingly examine thyself severely; peer into thy secret depths; and, whatever thou findest wrong in thee, by a vigorous reproof smite it, lay it low, bruise it, crush it, fling it from thee and annihilate it. Spare not thyself, flatter not thyself; but in the light of the morning--that is to say, in the view of the last assize, which, like the morning beam, is breaking on the night of this present life--slay all the sinners of the land--that is to say, the sins and delinquencies of thine earthly life--and so destroy out of the city of God which thou shouldest build to Him in thyself all those that work iniquity--that is, all diabolical suggestions, all delights hateful to God, all deadly consents, all froward acts. From all of them must thou, as the city of God, be thoroughly cleansed, that thus thy Creator may find, possess, and keep in thee an abode pleasing to Himself. Be not of those whose obstinacy very God seems to bewail when He says, There is none that considereth in his heart, and saith, What have I done?' (Is. lvii. 1.) If they are to be cast away who have refused to blush, and to accuse themselves for the sins they have committed, canst thou neglect to arraign, to judge, and with strict discipline chastise thyself? Review, then, in careful thought the innumerable blessings wherewith thy Creator has ennobled thee, no merits of thine own intervening, and call to mind thine own unnumbered evils, thy sole response--O, how wicked and how undeserved! for all those His benefits; and cry out in the pangs of a great grief, What have I done? Provoked my God, challenged my Creator's anger, repaid Him innumerable ills for untold goods. What have I done?' And speaking thus, rend, rend thy heart, pour forth sighs, weep showers of tears. For if thou weepest not here, when wilt thou weep?

And if the averted Face of God do not excite thee to contrition--a Face averted from thy sins--at least let the intolerable pains of hell, which those sins have provoked, break thy hard heart.

Return then, sinful soul, return into thyself. Draw thy foot out of hell; so mayest thou escape from the evils due to thee, and recover the lost goods of which thou art so justly bereft; for if thou revert with pleasure to thine own evils, then all the goods given thee by Him are lost and thrown away. It behoves thee, therefore, ever to keep a strict eye upon them, and chiefly those of which thy conscience does the more bitterly accuse thee, that so He may turn away His eye of anger from them. For if thou turnest aside thy sins with a due intention of satisfying for them, He turns aside His glance of retribution. If thou forgettest, He remembers.

[§ 8.] VIII. A review of our Lord's Incarnation, by means of which we have recovered all these losses. And that them mayest be set free from them, think of the compassions of thy Redeemer towards thee. Of a truth thou wast blinded by the guilt of original sin, and couldest not scan thy Creator's royal heights. Sins like a fog enveloped thee; thou wast drifting to the realms of darkness, and, swept on by the

15

whirling current of thy faults, thou wast hurrying to the eternal glooms; when lo, thy Redeemer applied the eye-salve of His Incarnation to thy blinded orbs, so that, albeit thou couldest not discern God shining in the secret chamber of His Majesty, thou mightest at any rate behold Him made manifest in man; and beholding, own; and owning, love; and loving, strive with all thy might to arrive at last at His glory. He was Incarnate to recall thee to a spiritual state; He became partaker of thy changeful lot to make thee sharer of His immutability; He stooped to thy lowliness that He might raise thee to His heights.

He was born of virginal integrity in order to heal the corruption of our wayward nature; circumcised, to teach man the duty of cutting away all excesses, whether of sin or of frailty; and offered in the temple and fondled by a holy widow, to teach His faithful to frequent the house of God, and aim by the pursuit of sanctity to merit to receive Him to themselves. He was embraced by the aged Simeon, who sang His praise, that so He might display to us His love of sober life and ripened character; and baptized, that thus He might sanctify for us the Sacrament of Baptism. And when in the Jordan, stooping to baptism at the hand of John, He heard the Voice of the Father, and received the Holy Spirit's advent under the figure of a dove, it was to teach us how to stand in unvarying humility of soul--as is intimated by the Jordan, which is by interpretation their going down--and so be favoured with converse with our heavenly Father, of Whom it is said, that His communication is with the simple' (Prov. iii. 32), and exalted by the presence of the Holy Ghost, Who takes His rest with the humble; at the hand of John withal, a name signifying the grace of God, that, whatever we receive from God, we ascribe all to His grace, not our merits. And when He had completed His fast of forty days, and was gloriously tended by ministrant angels, He taught us how, by turning away from the enticements of transitory things, all through the course of the present life to trample the world and the prince of the world under our feet, and so be guarded by troops of angels. By day He converses with the people, preaching the Kingdom of God to them, and edifies the surging crowds by His miracles and His doctrine; by night He frequents the mountain, and spends the time in prayer: hinting to us how, at one time, as opportunity offers, to point the way of life, according to our measure, by word and by example to our neighbours among whom we live; how at another, to betake ourselves to thoughtful solitude, and climb the hill of virtues, and yearn after the sweetnesses of high contemplation, and with unweariable desire direct our soul's bent to the things that are above. 'Tis on the mountain that He is transfigured before Peter and James and John; thus hinting to us that if like Peter (which is interpreted acknowledging) we humbly acknowledge our infirmity, if we endeavour to be made supplanters of vices (for James, or Jacobus, means supplanter), and strive faithfully to yield ourselves to the grace of God (for this is signified by the name of John), we shall climb all happily that heavenly mountain, and be hold the glory of Jesus; Jesus our King Himself being our Guide. 'Twas in Bethany that He woke Lazarus out of sleep (Bethany is interpreted the house of obedience); showing thus that all who by the effort of a right will die to this world and rest in the bosom of obedience, shall be wakened up by Him to everlasting life. Intrusting His Body and Blood to His disciples in the mystic supper, He humbly washed their feet; teaching us that the dread ministries of the altar must be celebrated with purity of deed and pious humility of mind. And then, or ever He was exalted in the glory of His holy resurrection, He endured the jests and the rough speeches of perfidious men, the shame of the Cross, the bitterness of gall, and at last death; in all this admonishing His own, that they who desire to attain after death to glory should not only endure with even mind the toils and distresses of the present life, and the oppressions of the wicked, but should love all hardnesses that this world can give, for the sake of guerdons through eternity; should love them, court them, and thankfully embrace them.

These, therefore, so glorious and countless benefits of thy Creator, if thou endeavour to ponder them worthily, to embrace them devoutly, and to imitate them with a fervent love, not only shalt thou recover the good things lost to thee through thy first parent, but by the unspeakable grace of thy Saviour thou shalt have far higher goods for thy possession through eternity. For thine own very God being made thy Brother by the mystery of the Incarnation, what unspeakable joy has He not insured thee against the day when thou shalt see thy nature exalted in His Person over all creation!

[§ 9.] IX. The duty of praying to be drawn out of the pit of misery and the mire of dregs. What then remains but, duly considering all these things, by all means possible to rouse thy heart's ardours towards the attainment of so great blessings, and to implore Him who created thee for their possession to snatch thee out of the pit of misery and out of the mire of dregs, and to make thee possessor of so great happiness? For what is the pit of misery' but the gulf of worldly desire? And what is the mire of dregs' but the filth of carnal pleasure?

For these, that is to say cupidity and pleasure, are two bands or leashes by which the human race is checked and held back lest it should attain the blessed liberty of heavenly contemplation. For in truth earthly desire is a pit of misery, a pit which engulfs the soul it has enthralled by numberless desires, and drags, as strongly as ever chains could drag, into a deep, a gulf of vices; and then allows her to have no rest. For the mind of man, once crushed by the yoke of cupidity, is dissipated from without by the love of visible things, and distracted from within by conflicting passions. Toil in acquiring, anxiety in multiplying, delight in possessing, fear of losing, distress at having lost; these all make havoc of her, nor do they allow her to see what danger she is in. This is the pit of misery, and these are the ills with which worldly cupidity for ever stores it. From this pit it was that the blessed David rejoiced that he had been rescued, when he broke forth into thanksgiving, and exclaimed, He hath brought me out of the pit of misery and the mire of dregs' (Ps. xxxix. 3). And the mire of dregs,' what is that? It is the delight of unchaste pleasure. Cry aloud, then, with the blessed David, and say to thy Creator, Draw me out of the mire, that I may not stick fast' (Ps. lxviii. 15). Cleanse thy heart from every stain of carnal delight, shut out impure musings from thy soul, if thou dost really long to get free out of the filth of this mire. But when by penance, by confession, by tears, by carefully inviting holy thoughts into the heart, thou hast clean escaped, then be ware that thou fall not back; but from the deep of thy heart of hearts sigh thou in the sight of God, and implore His mercy that He would set thy feet upon the rock; ask Him, that is to say, to establish thy heart's affections in the strength of Christ; that thy mind may root itself on the solid ground of justice, clinging inseparably to Christ, of whom, it is said that He is made unto us of God wisdom and justice and sanctification' (1 Cor. i. 30). Pray Him also to direct thy steps that they turn not back to sins, but may advance with unvarying course and inflexible intent in the way of His. heavenly precepts, and may hasten on with full determination to the angels' þlissful home.

But, in aspiring to such a goal as this, be not remiss in praising thy Creator; rather supplicate His mercy that He would put a new song in thy mouth, and help thee to sing with due devotion a hymn to our God. For it is meet that a soul united to God in a new life should ever sing a new song in His praise, despising temporal things and yearning only for eternal; obeying the Divine law now no more from fear of punishment, but from love of justice. For the singing of the new song to God is this, to crush the desires of the old man, and with thy whole heart's endeavour, and with a sole desire of eternal life, to walk the ways of the new man which have been pointed out to the world by the Son of God. And he sings a hymn to God who treasures in pure mind's recollection the joys of that heavenly home, and strives to reach them, supported by the consciousness of a holy life, and relying on the gift of supernatural grace.

[§ 10.] X. A consideration of the miseries of the present life. But withal, weigh well the miseries of the present life, and with watchful heart reflect how very cautiously thou shouldest live in it. Remember that thou art partaker of his lot of whom Scripture says, A man whose way is hidden, and God hath surrounded him with darkness' (Job iii. 23). For thou art indeed encompassed with a thick cloud of blind ignorance, since thou knowest not how God forms His estimate of thy works, and art all ignorant of the end that awaits thee. Man knoweth not,' says Solomon, whether he be worthy of love or hatred' (Eccles. ix. 1).

Picture to thyself some profound and darksome valley, stored in its depths with every kind of torments. High above it imagine a bridge, a solitary bridge, spanning the vast chasm, and measuring no more than a foot in breadth. This bridge, so narrow, so high, so perilous, if any one were forced to cross it whose eyes were bandaged so as not to see where he stepped, and his hands tied behind him so that he could not even grope with a staff to guide himself; what fear, think you, what perplexity would he not feel! What! Would there be place left in him for gaiety, for merriment, for wantonness? No, no, I warrant thee. All his pride would be taken from him, his vain-glory would be put to flight, and death, only death, would wave its dark shadow on his soul. Imagine, farther, hideous ravenous birds careering round the bridge, bent on dragging the traveller down into the deep; will not his terror be enhanced? And if, as he crosses, the boards are slipped ever from his heels, will he not be stricken with fresh alarms the further he advances?

But lay to heart the meaning of a similitude like this, and roused to solicitude brace thy mind with a godly fear. By that profound and dark some valley understand hell, hell deep and fathomless, and frightfully black with dreary gloom. Thither converge all kinds of torment; there all that soothes is not, all that terrifies, or tortures, or can distress, is, is everywhere. That perilous bridge, from which the awkward traveller launches headlong, is the present life, whence he who lives amiss falls and plunges into hell. The boards withdrawn at the passenger's heel are the several days of our life, which so pass away as never to return; but by the diminution of their number urge us to our destiny and compel us to hurry to our end. The birds wheeling about the bridge and waylaying those who cross it are malignant spirits, whose whole study is to cast men down from the straight way they are on, and to hurl them into the depths of hell. We, we are the passengers, blinded by the gloom of uncertainty, and, from the difficulty of doing right, clogged, as it were, with a heavy chain, so that we cannot tread the way of a holy life unfettered unto God. Consider, then, whether in so great danger thou must not cry with utmost earnestness to thy Creator, that, shielded by His protection, thou mayest sing with confidence while passing through the troops of the adversaries, The Lord is my light and my salvation, whom shall I fear?' (Ps. xxvi. 1.) Light, I mean, against blindness, salvation against danger; for these are the two evils in which our first parent has involved us, ignorance and danger; such ignorance and such danger that we neither know whither we are going nor what we are to do; and that, when we have after a sort seen where we are, even then, clogged and hampered by difficulty, we can not fully do that which we rightly know.

Dwell on these things, O my soul; muse upon them; let thy mind day by day practise herself therein. Intent on them, let her recall herself from anxieties and thoughts about useless objects, and inflame herself with the fire of a holy fear and a blessed love, that she may avoid these ills, and se cure eternal goods.

[§ 11.] XI. Of the body after the soul's departure. And now I return to Thee, most sweet Creator and most kind Redeemer, who hast made me and re-made me; and with lowly prayers I supplicate Thy pity, that Thou wouldest teach my heart to consider with life-giving fear and salutary alarms, in how loathsome and deplorable plight my flesh must be given over after death a prey to worms and putrefaction, bereft of the breath that now inspires it. Where then will be the beauty, if any it have, of which it boasts now? Where the exquisite delights it revels in? Where its pampered limbs? Will not the prophet's word then have its true fulfilment: All flesh is grass, and all the glory thereof as the flower of the field'? (Is. xl. 6.) My eyes will be shut, their orbs twisted in the socket; eyes from whose vain and mischievous wanderings I ofttimes drew pleasure. So shall they lie, covered over with fearful darkness; eyes that now love to drink in vanities as they drink in the light. My ears will lie exposed, soon to be crowded with worms; ears which now catch with an accursed delight slanderous speeches and the vain tittle-tattle of the world. My jaws, which gluttony has opened wide, will be tied up, miser ably locked together. My nostrils, which are now gratified with divers odours, will waste and rot away. My lips, which loved ever to be relaxed with silly laughter, will grin with rank unsightliness. My tongue, which has so often uttered idle stories, will be clogged with putrid foulness. And, what now are oft-times gorged with various kinds of meat, throat and belly, will be choked with worms, surfeited with worms! But why rehearse in detail? The whole frame and structure of the body, for the health, the comfort, and the pleasure of which almost every thought stands minister, will be dissolved into putrefaction and the worm, and last of all, vile dust. Where then the proud neck? Where the ornaments, the dress, the varied dainties? They are vanished, and gone like a dreamy gone all of them, never to return; and I, their poor, poor votary, left behind.

[§ 12.] XII. Of the soul after her separation from the body. O good God, what do I behold? Lo, fear meets fear, and grief encounters grief!

After her separation from the body, will not the soul be stormed by a multitude of demons flying to confront her, and charged to lay against her accusation upon accusation, indictment on indictment? And will not the soul be examined on all of these, down to the most trivial negligence? The prince of this world surrounded by his satellites will come, furious with rage; that prince so adroit in circumventing, so unscrupulous in lying, so spiteful in accusing; he will come, preferring against her, out of all her offences done, as many true charges as he can, and forging many false besides. O dreadful hour! O terrible ordeal! Here the rigorous Judge to judge me, there the pert adversaries to accuse me. My soul shall stand alone without a comforter, and with no source of solace, unless it be that the memory of its good works protects it.

But in so strict a reckoning, when all things shall be naked and open, who shall boast that he hath a chaste heart?' For if the just man shall scarcely be saved, where shall the ungodly and the sinner appear?' (1 St. Pet. iv. 18.) Then shall the lips of the flatterers fail; the fawning tongue shall wag no more, vain-glory shall be proved a traitor, false joys shall flee away, dignities and pomp shall take to flight, and the greed of power shall be seen to have been a hollow cheat. Happy then the soul which in such peril is protected by the consciousness of innocence, and shielded by the memory of holiness; happy the soul which, while as yet in her lodging of flesh, was over and over again washed with the waters of contrition, dressed and trimmed with careful confessions, and illuminated with the light of sacred meditations; happy the soul which had been chastened by humility, tranquillised by patience, detached from her own will by obedience, and inspired by charity to the exercise of all virtue. Such a soul will have no dread of that fearful hour, nor shall it be confounded when it shall speak to its enemies in the gate' (Ps. cxxvi. 5). For it will be joined to those of whom Scripture says, When He shall give sleep to His beloved, behold the inheritance of the Lord' (ib. 3).

[§ 13.] XIII. A consideration of the day of judgment, when the goats shall be set on the left hand. And now who can skill to say anything of the terrors of that last assize, when the sheep shall be set on the right hand, and the goats on the left? What will be the trembling when the powers of heaven shall be moved? What the crash of the elements, what the wailings, what the cries, when that terrible sentence shall be passed upon the careless ones, Depart from Me, you cursed, into everlasting fire' (St. Matt. xxv. 41). A day of wrath that day will be--dies iræ, dies illa--a day of tribulation and anguish, a day of clouds and whirlwind, a day of trumpet and the trumpet-blast! The voice of that day will be a bitter voice, and then the mighty shall be harrowed up; for they who now in the pride of their heart despise the will of God, and glory in the pursuit of their own self-will, shall then be wrapt in perpetual inextinguishable flame, and the undying worm shall feed on them, and the smoke of their torment shall go up for ever and ever.

[§ 14.] XIV. A consideration of the joy when the sheep shall be set on the right hand. But, while these are wailing and roaring out their heart's grief for anguish of spirit, what, thinkest thou, will be the happiness and exultation of those blessed ones, who, set on the right hand of God, are to hear His that most joyful summons, Come, ye blessed of My Father: possess you the Kingdom prepared for you from the foundation of the world' (St. Matt. xxv. 34). Then indeed shall the voice of joy and salvation dwell in the tabernacle of the just; then shall the Lord lift up the heads of the lowly, who now refuse not to be the vile and the outcast for His sake. He will heal the contrite of heart, and console with unending joys, according to their desire, those who now sorrow in their pilgrim age. Then will be seen the ineffable reward of those who held it joy to have thrown away their own wills from love of their Creator. In that day He will wreathe the heads of His obedient ones with a heavenly crown, and the glory of those who suffered shall shine forth with unutterable brightness. Then shall charity enrich her vassals with the society of all the angels, and purity of heart beatify her lovers with the all-happy vision of their Creator. Then shall God Himself reveal Himself to all who love Him, and raise them up for ever to enduring resting places and perpetual peace. Then in its truth shall this song be sung by all the elect: Blessed are they that dwell in Thy house; they shall praise Thee for ever and ever' (Ps. lxxxiii. 3). In which praise may He vouchsafe to give us a part, who with the Father and the Holy Ghost liveth and reigneth God for ever and ever. Amen.

SECOND MEDITATION

OF THE AWFUL JUDGMENT: FOR AWAKENING FEAR IN ONESELF.

[§ 15. The sinner's fear.] My life affrights me. For when carefully reviewed, its whole course shows in my sight like one great sin; or at least it is well-nigh nothing but barrenness. Or, if any fruit is seen in it, that fruit is so false, or so imperfect, or in some way or other so tainted with decay and corruption, that it must needs either fail to satisfy God, or else utterly offend Him.

So then, sinner, thy life, so far from being almost all, is altogether all steeped in sin, and therefore worthy of condemnation; or else it is unfruitful, and deserving of disdain. But why distinguish the unfruitful from the damnable? For surely, if it is unfruitful, it is damnable by that very fact. For what the Truth hath spoken is as evident as it is true: Every tree that doth not yield good fruit shall be cut down and cast into the fire' (St. Matt. iii. 10). For if I employ myself in constructing something useful or serviceable, surely I do not value the result of my labour at the price of the bodily sustenance which I consume while employed on the work. Who feeds a flock, pray, which is to bring in less than the value of its pasturage? And yet Thou, O God, Thou dost all too bountifully feed and foster me; and dost await me, good-for-nothing worm and foul sinner that I am. O, how less offensive is a dead dog to the human senses than a sinful soul is to God; how much more loathsome to God is this than that is to men! Ah, no; call not the sinner a man, but a reproach, a disgrace to humanity; viler than a brute, more odious than a carcase. My soul is aweary of my life; I am ashamed to live; I am afraid to die.

What, then, remains for thee to do, O sinner, but all through thy whole life to bewail thy whole life, and in such wise to do so as that all thy whole life may be a bewailing of itself?

But here again my soul is sadly bewildered, and bewilderingly sad as well; for it grieves not in proportion to its knowledge of itself, but slumbers on in such security as if it knew not in what plight it is. O barren soul, what art thou doing? O sinful soul, why dost thou slumber? The day of judgment is coming, the great day of the Lord is at hand; at hand, I say, and all too swift. The day of wrath that day shall be; the day of tribulation and anguish, the day of calamity and misery, the day of darkness and gloom, the day of cloud and whirl-wind, the day of trumpet and the trumpet-cry. O bitter voice of the day of God! Why dost thou slumber, thou lukewarm soul? thing neither hot nor cold, and fit only to be vomited out of the mouth, why dost thou slumber? He that awakes not, he that trembles not, at such thunders is not asleep but dead. O barren tree, where are thy fruits? Tree fit only for the axe and the fire, fit to be cut down and burnt, what are thy fruits? Why, they are only pricking thorns and bitter sins I Would to God the thorns pricked thee to repentance and so got broken; would to God those bitter fruits dropped off and perished!

Perhaps thou thinkest some sin or other a little thing. Would that thy strict Judge thought any sin a little thing! But, ah me, does not every sin by its unholiness dishonour God? What then; will the sinner dare to call a sin a little thing? When is it a little thing to dishonour God? O dry and useless tree, worthy of eternal flames, what wilt thou answer in that day when a strict account, down to the twinkling of an eye, shall be required of thee of all the time dealt out to thee for living in, as to how it has been spent by thee? Ay, then will be condemned whatsoever shall be found in thee of labour or of leisure, of speech or of silence, down to the slightest thought; even the very fact that thou hast lived; if that life has not been ruled and directed to the will of God. Alas, how many sins will then start into view, as from an ambush, which now thou seest not! More, assuredly, and more terrible, it may be, than those which thou now seest. How many things which thou now thinkest not at all wicked, how many which thou now believest to be good, will then stand forth unmasked, sins of the deepest, blackest die! Then without doubt thou wilt receive according as thou hast done in the body; then, when there shall be no more time of mercy; then, when no repentance shall be accepted, when no promise of amendment may be made.

Here reflect on what thou hast done, and what award thou must receive. If much good and little evil, rejoice much; if much evil and little good, grieve much. What! O good-for-nothing sinner, are not thy evil deeds enough to extort a great and bitter cry? Are they not enough to distil thy blood and thy marrow into tears? Wo to the strange hardness, which such heavy hammers are too light to break! O, insensible torpor, that such sharp goads are not sharp enough to waken! Alas for the deadly sleep, that thunders so terrific are too dumb

25

to startle! O worthless sinner, all this should be enough to prolong a ceaseless grief; and surely it is enough to draw perpetual tears!

But why should I smother in silence aught of the weight or of the magnitude of the misery that threatens? Why cheat the eyes of my soul? Shall I do so, that sudden sorrow may rain all unforeseen on the sinner; or that the intolerable storm may pelt upon him unawares? Surely this is riot for his interest. But if I should put into words whatever I might contrive to conjure up in imagination, yet that could never bear any sort of comparison with the reality.

Therefore let my eyes drop tears all day and all night, and never rest. Come, sinner, come; add fresh griefs to thy load of griefs; add terror to terror; add cry to cry; for He the very God will judge thee, in despite of whom I sin in every act of disobedience, and in every waywardness; He who has returned me good for evil, whilst I have given Him evil for good; who is now most long-suffering, but will then be most severe; who is now most merciful, and will then be most just.

Wo is me! wo is me! Against Whom have I sinned? I have dishonoured God; provoked the Omnipotent. Sinner that I am, what have I done! Against Whom have I done it! How wickedly have I done it! Alas, alas! O wrath of the Omnipotent, fall not on me; wrath of the Omnipotent, where could I endure thee? There is no place in all of me that could bear thy weight. O anguish! Here, sins accusing; there, justice terrifying; beneath, the yawning frightful pit of hell; above, an angry Judge; within, a burning conscience; around, a flaming universe! The just will scarcely be saved; and the sinner entangled thus, whither, whither shall he fly? Tight bound, where shall I crouch and cower; how shall I show my face? To hide will be impossible, to appear will be intolerable; I shall long for the one, and it is nowhere; I shall loathe the other, and it is everywhere! What then? what then? What will happen then? Who will snatch me from the hands of God? Where shall I find counsel, where shall I find salvation? Who is He that is called the Angel of great counsel, that is called the Saviour, that I may shriek His Name? Why, here He is; here He is; it is Jesus, Jesus the very Judge Himself, in whose hands I am trembling!

[§ 16. The sinners hope.] Breathe again, sinner, breathe again; do not despair; trust in Him. thou fearest. Fly home to Him from

Whom thou hast fled away; cry cravingly to Him Whom thou hast so proudly provoked. Jesus, Jesus; for the sake of this Thy Name, deal with me according to this Name. Jesus, Jesus; forget Thy proud provoker, and bend Thine eye upon the poor invoker of Thy Name, the Name so sweet, the Name so dear, the Name so full of comfort to a sinner, and so full of blessed hope. For what is Jesus but Saviour? Therefore, Jesus, for Thine own self's sake be a Jesus to me; Thou who formedst me r that I perish not; who redeemedst me, that Thou condemn me not; who createdst me by Thy goodness, that Thy handiwork perish not by my iniquity. Recognise and own, Benignest, what is Thine; take away what is another's. Jesus, Jesus r mercy on me, while the day of mercy lasts, that Thou damn me not in the day of judgment. For what profit shalt Thou have in my blood, if I go down into eternal corruption? For the dead shall not praise Thee, O Lord, nor any of them that go down to hell' (Ps. cxiii. 17). If Thou fold me in the wide, wide Bosom of Thy mercy, that Bosom will be none the less wide on my account. Therefore admit me, O most desired Jesus, admit me into the number of Thine elect; that with them I may praise Thee, and enjoy Thee, and make my boast in Thee amongst all who love Thy Name; who with the Father and the Holy Ghost reignest gloriously throughout unending ages. Amen.

27

THIRD MEDITATION

A BEMOANING OF VIRGINITY SADLY LOST.

[§ 17. The sinner's past.] O my soul, O woe begone soul, O wretched soul of an all too wretched mortal, throw aside thy lethargy, throw away thy sin, throw into thy task all the powers of thy mind; call home to heart thine outrageous guilt, and from that heart call forth a wild and woeful cry. Be think thee, wretch, bethink thee of thy horrible crime; prolong thy horror-stricken terror and thy terror-stricken grief. For thou, thou that once wast washed white in the celestial bath, dowered with the Holy Ghost, vowed in Christian profession; thou wast a virgin betrothed to Christ. O, where does memory lead me! O, whose is this Name I name! He is now no longer the loving Spouse of my virginity, but the terrible Judge of my unchastity. Ah, memory of lost happiness, why dost thou thus aggravate afresh the burden of the woe that masters me? How sad the plight of a man debauched, to whom good and ill alike are a torture! For an evil conscience racks me, and those its threatened torments in which I fear that I shall burn; and the memory of a good conscience racks me, and the thought of those its rewards which I know that I have lost, and shall never more recover. O sad, O grievous loss; the loss of losing irrecoverably that which ought to be interminably kept; an inconsolable loss, alas! a losing that has not only foredone my blessings, but has won me fresh racks and torments.

O virginity, now no longer my loved, but my lost; now no more a delight, but a despair to me; whither art thou gone? What rank salt mire is this where thou hast left me? And thou, fornication, mind's polluter, soul's destroyer, whence didst thou creep and steal on wretched me? And O, from how bright and glad a standing-place hast thou hurled me down! Here thou with thy fever parchest me, O bitter woe, for I have let go the one; and here thou, O irksome grief, and fear of a worse yet, dost torture me, for I have let the other come. On the one hand in consolable loss, on the other intolerable torment. Woe on this side, and woe again on that! Thus equally, O good and evil, thus with exactest justice do ye both punish miserable, wicked me, even while I live. Deservedly, deservedly indeed. For thou, O my soul, faithless to God, foresworn to God, false spouse of Christ, hast deliberately dropped from thy virgin height, and miserably plunged into the gulf of fornication. Thou, that wast erst espoused to the King of heaven, hast made thyself mistress to the gaoler of hell. Ah, soul, cast away from God, cast forth to the devil; rather caster away of God and embracer of the devil. The act was thine, O my miserable soul; for 'twas thine, 'twas thine, become a brazen strumpet and a shameless courtesan, to give bill of divorce to thy Lover and thy Creator God, and bestow thyself on thy seducer and destroyer demon. O wretched, wretched change!

Alas, from what a height hast thou fallen, into what an abyss hast thou been hurled! Fie upon thee; thou hast scorned One, O how kind; and linked thee to one, O how malignant! What hast thou done, O madness, O unchastity all too mad, O wickedness all too unchaste? Thou hast left thy chaste Lover in heaven, and followed thy hateful seducer into hell, and prepared thee in hell's pit a filthy lair in place of thy bridal chamber. Astounding horror, what perversity of will is this! Miracle of horror, what wilful perversity is this! Whence, then, O God, am I to draw for myself the corrective of such deep depravity? whence for Thee, O God, satisfaction for so black a sin? Fling thyself, miserable mortal, down into the black abyss of a woe unmedicined, thou that didst choose to fling thyself into the pit of a horrible iniquity. Wrap thee about, poor wretch, in guise of terrible grief, thou that didst all willingly launch into the slime of hellish filth. And thou, steeped in crime, muffle thyself round with horrid glooms of inconsolable wailing, thou that didst wanton wilfully in the quagmire of so grovel ling indulgence. Wallow in the gulf of bitterness, thou that didst dally in the bed of shame.

O shrinking terror, trembling grief, inconsolable distress, crowd, crowd upon me; whelm me, overwhelm me, bewilder me, encompass me, and make me all your own. 'Tis just, 'tis just. I have flouted you by my shameless daring; I have provoked you by my filthy wantonness no, no, God; God, not you and now in woebegone repentance I desire you. Torture your victim; avenge your God; let the fornicator feel betimes the hell-torment he has merited; let him have a foretaste of what he has laid up for himself; let him get accustomed to what he has to suffer. Prolong and lengthen out thy doleful penance, thou uncontrolled, unbridled sinner, that didst so long prolong thy impurity and thy guilt. Roll back, roll back into the same seething gulf of bitterness, thou that didst so oft roll back into the same slough of lusts. And as for you, consolation, security, and joy, I forego you, I reject you till pardon of sin restore you. Away with you, away with you, before I die; if haply forgiveness may recall you to me, albeit after death. Let perpetual penance be the sad companion of my time; let perpetual grief be the unsatisfied torturer of my life; let sadness and harsh mournfulness be the unfatigued harrowers-up of my early and my latter age. O be it so! O be it so! I desire, I pray, I long that it may be so. For though I am unworthy to lift my eyes to heaven in prayers, surely I am not unworthy to blind them with tears. If my mind from shame of conscience is too much confounded to pray, 'tis right it should be confounded by the giddy bewilderment that comes of a mourner's distress and grief. If it fears to be displayed in the sight of God, 'tis just it should have in its own sight the torments that its guilt has earned.

[§ 18. The sinner's future.] So, then, let my heart ponder and ponder again on what it has done and what it has deserved. Let my mind go down, yes, down to the land of darkness, the land covered with the shadow of death; and there let her scan the torments that await a guilty soul; let her gaze on them, and study them; let her see, and be sore troubled. What is it, O God, what is it that I descry in the land of misery and darkness? Horror, horror! What is it that I behold here, where no order, but everlasting horror dwelleth? (Job x. 22.) Ah, the jarring shrieks, the tears and hurly-burly, the gnashing of teeth, the disordered advance of multitudinous wailings, wo, and wo; how many wo's! how many and how many wo's, and wo's on the heels of wo's! Ah, the sulphurous fire, the flame from the nether most deep! You volumes of blackest smoke, with what frightful roaring do I see you wreathe and roll! You worms, alive in fire; what strange appetite for gnawing thus inflames you, you that the fire of fires does not burn? And you, ye demons, glowing through and through, chafing with rage, gnashing your teeth with frenzy, why are ye so merciless to them that are writhing in the midst of you? O all and every kind of torments, measured by justice, but measureless to power of endurance, is it so that no controlment, no respite, no end is ever to subdue you? Are these the things, great God, that have been prepared for fornicators and despisers of Thee, of whom I am one? I, yes I; I am one of them.

Shudder, O my soul; and faint, my mind; and break, my heart. Whither do you drag me, O punishers of my guilt? Whither dost thou thrust me, O my sin? Whither dost thou drive me, O my God? If I have contrived to be Thy culprit, say, could I have contrived not to be Thy creature? If I have robbed me of my chastity, say, have I bereft Thee of Thy mercy? O Lord, O Lord, if I have let that come whence

Thou canst damn, hast Thou let that go whence Thou art wont to save? Do not, do not, O Lord, so look upon my evil as to forget Thy good. Where, where, O God of truth, is that Thy, I desire not the death of the sinner, but that the sinner turn from his way and live'? (Ezech. xxxiii. 11.) O Lord, who liest not, O Lord, what means Thy nolo mortem peccatoris, if Thou bury down in hell a sinner crying unto Thee? To plunge a sinner into the bottomless pit, is this Thy volo ut convertatur, Thy volo ut vivat? I am the sinner, O Lord, I am the sinner. If, then, Thou desirest not the death of the sinner, what forces Thee to do what Thou desirest not, to give me over to the death? If Thou desirest that the sinner turn again and live, what prevents Thee from doing what Thou dost desire, that Thou convert me, and I live? What! does the enormity of my sin force Thee to what Thou desirest not, although Thou art Almighty God? Forbid it, Almighty God; forbid it, O Lord God; let not the wickedness of a sinner, a confessing, grieving sinner, prevail against the decree of the Omnipotent.

Remember, O just, O holy, O bountiful God, that Thou art merciful, and hast made me and re-made me. Therefore remember not, good Lord, Thy justice against Thy sinner, but be mindful of Thy condescension to Thy creature; remember not Thy fury against the guilty, but be mindful of Thy mercy to the miserable. True it is that my conscience and sense of guilt deserves damnation, and that my penance is not enough for satisfaction; but yet it is certain that Thy mercy out strips all Thy resentment. Spare, therefore, Thou good Lord, to whom salvation belongeth, and who desirest not the death of the sinner, spare my sinful soul; for it flies, frightened by Thy frightening justice, to Thy consoling mercy; that so, since the treasure of his marred virginity is now--O grief!--irrecoverable, yet the punishment due to fornication may not be inevitable to the penitent; for 'tis neither impossible to Thy omnipotence, nor ill-becoming to Thy justice, nor unwonted to Thy mercy; since Thou art good, and since Thy mercy reaches to eternity, Thou who art blessed for ever more. Amen.

FOURTH MEDITATION

TEACHING THE SINNER TO BESTIR HIMSELF FOR THE AMENDMENT OF HIS SINS.

[**§ 19. The necessity and the benefit of careful self-examination.**] O soul of mine, so wretched and so soiled, recall to thee and carefully compose all thy bodily senses; and with more than usual care look and see how grievously thou art wounded and laid low. For since thy Creator, in His in finite goodness, grants thee life, since in His ineffable compassion He so patiently and all so tenderly awaits thy amendment, and a suitable satisfaction, be not slow and indolent in the curing of thy wounds, in the correcting of thy sins, in the reconciling of thy offended Creator, and in the making friends to thee of all His saints, whom by thy offences against their Creator and thine, their Lord and thine, thou hast turned into thy foes. If thou hadst always remained upright and pure, upright and pure as thy Creator made thee, if thou hadst always--as thou couldest well have done, hadst thou chosen--conformed thyself to His will without defection, thou wouldest now be running, happy and joyful, a happy and joyful course through this present life; the which course run through and finished, thou wouldest find assured to thee, happy and joyful, by His help, the possession of that happy and joyful life which has no end. But now, since, all wretched and unhappy, thou hast set at naught the will of thy Creator, and clung wretchedly and unhappily to thine own carnal pleasures; if, carefully refusing to pamper thyself, carefully refusing to spare thyself in what evils soever and what iniquities soever thou dost find that thou art entangled; if, seeing them and repenting of them, thou art setting thyself in earnest to return into the path of satisfaction and amendment; if so, then, by way of a beginning, throw away one thing from thine inmost self; I mean this, the willing inclination to sin; throw it away, and embrace and do what thou so well knowest will be pleasing to thy Creator.

But it may be that thou sayest to thyself, beholding the enormity of thy sins, and despairing of indulgence and remission--it may be that thou sayest, having regard to thy habitual offences and their foulness, How can I possibly henceforth have strength enough to amend my ways? I that am acting against the will of God, now well-nigh a lifetime; I whose whole being is set on the gratification of all kinds of wicked desires, and the doing of all kinds of wicked deeds; I that lie here hardened in sins, like some stone which iron cannot cut and fire cannot melt? For when with more than ordinary care I contemplate the justice of my Creator, and review the evil deeds which ever and anon I have committed, I am certain that nothing awaits me but the torments which evil deeds deserve.' True, true enough is what thou sayest; for God, just judge and lover of equity that He is, ordains torments as the punishment of sins and evil deeds. But nevertheless, according to the measure of that very justice which makes Him punish those who persist in wickedness, does He repay with an ever-enduring guerdon those w r ho repent of their evil deeds, and do what is good.

For this reason did I just now admonish thee to examine thine inmost parts and all thy doings in His sight with special care; and with no less care to fix thine eye on the issue to which thy doings tend. If thou persevere in this, and persevere too in bruising thy hard heart with hammers of iron, as it were, by these reviews--if so, I verily believe that thou wilt thus do what, unless thou art mad, will yield thee as its return happiness and endless joys, and wilt rid thyself of that whence thou hast been meriting misery and torments.

[§ 20. The goodness of God, and the malignity of the Devil.] For this reason do I again and yet again admonish thee unintermittingly to recollect how sweet and how good is thy Creator towards thee; how great was His goodness in creating thee when thou wast not, and in making thee, instead of a dumb brute or an insensible creature, a being such as could understand and love Him, and, joyful and eternal, share His eternity with Him; how great His goodness in loving thee with such excess of love as that, though He knew that thou wouldest do many things against His will, He yet re fused not to create thee, and lo, thou art; how great His goodness in awaiting thine amendment with such gentle forbearance, so mercifully and compassionately does He still bear with thee! Yes, He awaits; thy Creator awaits thy improvement, as I said;. for He who was pleased to make thee, never, never wishes to destroy thee; rather would He have thee return to His all-merciful compassion; rather would He reward thee, cleansed and amended by true repentance, with that happy and eternal life which thou hadst lost through sin.

Think, therefore, and think again and again, of thy Creator's kindness to thee; and, as is right, raise thyself and all thy powers to the contemplation of His unspeakable love. For the love of Him brooks no foulness of vice, and consents to no pleasure bred of carnal desires. For where love of Him reigns, there utmost peace abides, and deepest calm, and perfect readiness to do and think all that may tend to the attainment of eternal happiness. Know well that in all thy actions and all thy thoughts there are two round about thee, and very close to thee; one thy friend, the other thy foe. Thy friend is thy Creator, who rejoices in all thy good works; whilst thy foe, the devil, is mortified at those same good works of thine. The devil, ever laying snares for thee as he does, is rejoiced if he see thee do evil deeds, and give heed to vain and foolish thoughts, whence he may be able to find accusation against thee before the Great Judge, and drag thee, thus accused and hence condemned, down with himself into perdition. The devil, ever eager for the destruction of the faithful, not only accuses them of the ills they really do, he even tries to set a stain on their good deeds and their right thoughts by making out of them material for his false charges. But be thou, on thy side, upon thy guard against his subtle tricks, and against his wiles so full of all deception; be on thy guard, be solicitous; and call upon thy Creator and thy dearest Lord not to let thee be led astray by the wiles and the deceptions of the foe. O, fly under the shadow of His wings from the face of the wicked who afflict thee (Ps. xvi. 8, 9), and who make it their aim, having afflicted and supplanted thee, to drag thee away to death and eternal ruin. Thy Creator and thy Lord is merciful and compassionate, far, far beyond the reach of words or even thoughts; so much so, that never does He destroy any man but through the man's own great fault and own great sin.

[§ 21. The compassion of Jesus.] Earthly parents, father and mother, in our flesh, are wont to feel great compassion and sympathy for their offspring; and if they find them afflicted with pain of any kind, or any bodily inconvenience, are ready enough to spend both themselves and their fortunes, should reason so require, for their children's recovery to ease and soundness. Ofttimes, too, many dumb animals even do not shrink from facing death itself for their young; and only too willingly go to meet it, that their offspring may escape it. Whence, now, comes this to man and to the brute? Whence comes this natural sympathy, but from Him who is the Father of sympathy and compassion; who wills not that any should perish, and rejoices not in the destruction of them that die? Our Creator, therefore, the Fountain of compassion, the Fountain of mercy, when He sees us His children stained with any sinful contagion, or hurt well nigh to death with the many and deep wounds that crime has made, displays towards us greater devotion in curing our sins, in healing our sickness, in cleansing away the leprosy and filth of our misdeeds, in wiping out the soils of our vain thoughts, than does earthly father for his children, or reasonless brute for its young. Nor is it enough for Him simply to cure our sicknesses, and so dismiss us; when we are healed, He makes us His own close familiars, and afterwards folds us tenderly in His arms as His own dearest children; ay, He embraces us and kisses us, and then soothes and consoles away all our infirmities, and all the sinful leprosy we had contracted by our folly, and entirely forgets all the injuries we once did Him by spurning Him in His consolations. He clothes us with honour in this present life, and crowns us with glory in the next; He makes us kings; and, as to our soul, her He makes a queen, whence He admonishes us as kings, already made so in the psalm: And now, O ye kings, understand; receive instruction, you that judge the earth' (Ps. ii. 10). For we then are kings indeed, when we rule our inordinate motions, and reduce them to reason and the will of our Creator; we receive instruction when we judge the earth, that is to say, when, if we see that our heart desires earthly things, we compel it to contemn the earthly and to love the heavenly. Our soul becomes a queen; for arrayed in varied robes--that is to say, adorned with divers virtuous gifts--she is wedded in mind's continuous act and habit to Christ her Spouse who is in heaven, even whilst she sojourns here on earth. It was not enough for our Creator to create us, and to govern us when created, and to send angels, as often as need was, to defend us; but He in His own Person, taking our form to Him, taking our nature to Him, out of pity for the work of His hands, came down to us, looked carefully at our wounds, touched them, felt them; and, moved with pity for the misery which He saw enthralled us, grieved over us, and sighed in His inmost soul. He pitied, grieved, and sighed for us; and then of that very Flesh which He had assumed for our sake, made as it were a healing ointment, and applied it to our griefs, and restored us from our sickness back to perfect health. And, that He might in this mystery show how much He loved us, He gave us that very Flesh which He had assumed for us, that we might eat It; and onwards to this day fails not to administer It to us in the sacrifice of His altar. Thou, then, my soul, consoled and animated by the sweet recollection of all these mercies, pray to thy Lord, pray to thy Creator; invoke all His saints to thy assistance, that, aided and consoled by their intercession, thou mayest gain of Him who made thee grace so to live in this thy present state, so to purge away thy iniquities by true repentance and confession, as that, thy transitory passage run, thou mayest merit to mount up to joys eternal; by His help who liveth and reigneth God to eternal ages. Amen.

FIFTH MEDITATION

[§ 22] ON THE LIFE OF SOUL AND OF FLESH, [§ 23] AND OF
THE GLORY OF THE
GOOD SOUL, [§ 24] AND THE MISERY OF THE WICKED SOUL,
ON THEIR DEPARTURE FROM THE BODY.

So long as his soul dwells in the body, a man lives according to the flesh; and on its departure he dies according to the same flesh. And it is equally true that, just as the soul supplies life to the flesh so long as it remains in the flesh, so that flesh in turn supplies the soul with life so long as the flesh does the works of justice. Thus soul and flesh are seen to act reciprocally; the soul working for the flesh, and the flesh for the soul; and, pro vided that the soul cooperates duly with the flesh, they win for each other the life of an. enduring life. There is a difference, however; inasmuch as the soul is introduced to that life when it has shaken off the flesh, whereas the flesh will not enjoy it until reunited to that soul at the resurrection on the last day. Therefore rejoice, O my soul, and thou, my flesh, rejoice in the living God (Ps. lxxxiii. 3). Come ye to God your Creator; come, and be enlightened (Ps. xxxiii. 6); and now no longer do that of which ye should be ashamed; but always study to do what may ensure you joy for ever. I implore and I exhort you, that you receive not the grace of God in vain (2 Cor. vi. 1). For although He now suffers much to be done by you which much displeases Him, think not that He will suffer it always. For He is patient, doubtless, but yet a rewarder; and loving, but yet a searcher of heart and reins. He endures much now, awaiting our amendment, such is His great gentleness; but if we do not correct ourselves betimes, He will condemn us, such is His perfect justice. And He, who is now so kind to us as to call us His brethren and His friends, will then, at that last scrutiny, reject us as enemies whom He refuses to know, there being no good works by which He can know us.

My soul and my flesh, now, now at least, keep watch at all times and everywhere, thinking on your end. For, it may be, you will not easily sin if you do this; and, if you do it as I admonish you, you may be secure; because, in the day when many are sorrowing who now laugh and rejoice, you will be glad and exult with an unspeakable joy.

Give diligent heed, therefore, to your works. If they are good and pleasing to God, rejoice; if they are bad and not acceptable to Him, reform them at once. Let not your eye slumber, nor your eyelids sleep. The pit of perdition is wide open, .and he who is ever so little off his guard, slips into it easily enough. Sin, injustice, folly, vanity, impel him to it scarce resisting, and, once plunged into it, there will be no escaping for ever. But as the pit of eternal destruction yawns for the wicked and the evil workers, so the gate of Paradise stands opened wide to the good and those who persevere in goodness; and the soul once welcomed there shall always remain and dwell there, full of joy and gladness for ever and ever.

[§ 23.] And now let us trace, if we can, with careful eye the course by which good works raise to heaven the soul of him who has lived well, whilst evil works drag the soul of the sinner into hell. The purged soul, as soon as she parts from the body, sees all her works; and seeing that all of them are good, rejoices with an indescribable joy. Presently an angel takes her into his keeping; yes, the angel who guarded her eyes from beholding vanity, and closed her ears against hearing iniquity, he embraces her; who kept watch about her mouth, that it should not speak lies, he protects her; who shielded her from sinning by sense of touch or smell, he rejoices in her; and in his great joy and blithesomeness hovers round about her, and sets her before the throne of the Divine brightness, there to be happy without end. And other angels then fly to greet her, and other saints, whose post is there before the face of the Majesty of God, and recognising her as their friend and their associate in good works, joyfully embrace her with the arms of a tenderest love; and, ac costing her as follows, declare the common joy of one and all of the denizens of bliss: Lo, thou art our companion; lo, thou art our friend, for thou hast served God faithfully, and hast laboured with all thy might to do His commandments; now, now at last rest thee from thy toil, and enjoy unending happiness, now and onwards through eternity.'

[§ 24.] But, on the other hand, when the soul of the wicked is forced to go out of the body, angels of Satan presently receive her; and, binding her roughly with chains of fire, and forcing her still more roughly on from every side, hurry her off to the torments of that hell where Satan, plunged in the pit, lies deep and low, where there is weeping and gnashing of teeth (St. Matt. viii. 12), where fire and brimstone and storms of wind is the portion of the cup of sinners' (Ps.

x. 7). Then the infernal king, Satan himself, clutching her in his grasp, and belching on her a breath of loathsome fire, orders her to be pinioned by his satellites, and, thus bound, to be cast into the midst of the tormenting fires, there to be tortured with out end with them, there without end to die undyingly for very grief. Then the unhappy soul, racked with pains, hedged round by the infernal fiends, above, beneath, on every side, returning at last to herself, and seeing all the evils she has ever done, cries with a woful cry, Ah, poor me, poor me! why did I ever live? Poor me, racked all over with such strange torments! poor me! O worms, O worms, why do you gnaw me so cruelly? Pity me, pity me; pity poor me, that suffer so many and such awful other torments! Ah, poor me, poor me! And I want to die; but, dying and dying, still I cannot die. Now do I, poor wretch, receive again all wherein I sinned, by sight, by taste, by hearing, by smell, by touch.' And yet it avails not the woe-begone soul so miserably grieving, so late repenting, so sadly crying out for pain, that so great sorrow now afflicts it. No; what in her earthly life she merited, that she now receives in the pains of hell, poor soul, poor sinful soul.

Therefore pay good heed, O my soul, and thou, O my flesh; and paying heed, judge true judgment, and decide which is the better, which the more profitable, course to follow; to do well and receive good, or to do ill and receive evil? Unless you are fools, you will answer, To do well and get good.' Therefore do good; do good that you may be able to have good, that Good from which all good is; I mean the Good of all good, which cannot but be good. Our Creator has given us many good things, He has placed many within our reach; but there is no good so precious, none so worthy of every wise man's quest, as THE GOOD. to whom no created good may be compared; and He is our Creator Himself, who is never other than good. Which Good, if, by His grace, you are able to have, you will have all other goods in Him. But if, having others, you have not Him, the Sole Good, you labour in vain, and, like idiots chasing the wind, you will find at last not truth, but hollowness and vanity.

No; all present glory, as indeed you see it to be if you rightly consider the matter, is like a bladder filled with wind; which, so long as it is held in the hands quite carefully and only looked at, shows goodly and fair enough; but if by any chance the smallest hole be pricked in it, emptiness--not goodliness, only emptiness and wind--is left in your hands.

Therefore reflect; and, as I admonished you at the beginning of this meditation, think ever on your last end; because thus thinking, and being always solicitous about your departure hence, you will not easily sin; and so living on to the last, the temporal joys being ended, which, whilst you were thus timorous, flitted like a puff of wind across your cheek, you will find not vanity but truth, which is Christ; to whom may He bring you who created you. Amen.

SIXTH MEDITATION

DESIGNED TO BRACE THE HEART AGAINST DESPAIR, FORASMUCH AS WE SHALL WITHOUTDOUBT FIND TRUE MERCY FOR ALL OUR SINS IF WE DO TRUE PENANCE.

[**§ 25. The condition of the sinner.**] I feel no little fear when I look back upon the sins I have committed, and bethink me of the pains and torments which I deserve to suffer for them; and so, in my great anxiety and my great alarm lest I should be lost, I look about me to see if haply I may anywhere discover any means of consolation. But, alas poor me! I find none; for not only my Creator, but my Creator and the whole creation He has made, are, I know full well, enlisted as my adversaries. Thus my Creator with His whole creation, grievously offended at my sins, condemns me; whilst my conscience, too well assured of its evil deeds, accuses me at every point. So that I find no consolation, nor do I think that I shall readily procure it from any source whatever.

What, then, am I to do? Whither shall I turn, desolate as I am, entangled as I am in the meshes of my sins? If I resolve to turn again to Him who made me upright, and so supplicate His unspeakable mercy to have pity on me, I greatly fear lest by my so great rashness I should move Him to all the greater anger against me, and lest He should all the more severely on this account avenge Himself on those enormities of mine by the which I have not feared to provoke His loving-kindness.

What then? Am I to lie still, as though in despair, without counsel, without help? My Creator even now suffers me to live, even now fails not to supply me with all that is needful for the sustentation of this present life; and, for I find it by actual experience, my sins avail not to conquer His goodness, and induce Him to determine now at last to cover me with confusion, as I have long ago deserved, and destroy me altogether. Of all certainties this is most certain, that He is merciful to me, inasmuch as He lavishes on me such inestimable blessings, and that even now He does not seek to avenge Himself on my iniquities.

[**§ 26. The Divine mercy before the Incarnation.**] I have heard, and what I have heard is true--for they who have had experience of a fact are in a position to attest it--that He the Fountain of Mercy, which began to flow from the very be ginning of the world, flows still. He was abundantly merciful, as they tell us, and very pitiful to Adam our first father, in that He did not punish him forthwith with the eternal perdition he had deserved on committing that sin of eating the forbidden fruit; but patiently waited for his amendment, and gave him merciful helps to enable him to return into the grace of Him whom he had offended. Indeed, He often sent him and those who sprang from him angels, for this very end; admonishing them to return and do penance for their iniquities; for He was still willing to receive them, should they with all their hearts repent of their sins. But they, still persisting in their sins and despising His admonitions, added fresh sins to the old; and grown mad, as it were, frantic, and hateful in their iniquities, began against their nature, although created in honour by reason of God's likeness, to imitate the behaviour of brute beasts.

Then again He sent patriarchs, He sent prophets; but even then men chose not to forsake their crooked and perverse ways, but, of those who gave them counsels of salvation, slew some, and afflicted others with various and unheard-of tortures. Still, like a merciful father, He chastened them for a season, not to avenge Himself on their affronts and scorn, as though goaded to it by their evil deeds, but that they thus corrected might have recourse to His mercy, who in no wise desires the perdition of those whom He of His goodness created out of nothing.

[§ 27. The Divine mercy in the Incarnation.] But when, visited and visited again, first by admonition, then by correction, they still refused to be converted, the Fountain of Mercy could restrain Himself no longer, but, descending from the Bosom of the Father, took our true humanity, took our sinful likeness, and began all sweetly to admonish them that they should do salutary penance for their sins, and should own Him to be the very Son of God. For He had come for their salvation, and they must not lose hope, but must believe most firmly that pardon was now theirs for all their sins, if only they forsook them and did penance. For there is no sin so grievous that it cannot be washed out by penance, and so washed out as that the devil himself can no more henceforth call it to remembrance. Then, therefore, sinners beholding the so great sweetness of their Creator, began of their own accord to run in eager crowds to the Fountain of Mercy, and to wash away their sins in Him. Nay more; He on His part proceeded,

42

Fountain of Mercy, to live with sinners, proceeded to throw open to them the sacred doors of that sacramental confession by means of which every burden of sin is lightened and removed, for in true confession every stain is cleansed and washed away.

      After this, as the time drew near when He must suffer for the redemption of sinners, the Jews, of whose stock He was sprung according to the flesh, moved with envy for that He was merciful and compassionate, crucified Him. And yet He, even in His very death, not unmindful of His compassion, prayed to His Father for His murderers, that He would forgive them this sin, for they know not'--were His words--for they know not what they do' (St. Luke xxiii. 34). Thus does that sweetest compassion of our Lord find excuses for them; our Lord who desires not the death of the wicked, but that he turn from his way and live (Ezech. xxxiii. 11). Who, then, has heart so hard, so stony hard, that the so great loving-kindness of his Creator cannot soften it; whom, though His creature made by Him out of nothing to His image and likeness, he treated with dishonour; yet He punished not revengefully, but, dishonoured as He was and provoked by men's many evil deeds, yet endured all with patience, and sweetly admonished them to return to Him with out doubt and without delay. Ay, indeed; our Lord Jesus Christ is merciful and sweet; as where He says by His prophet, Is it my will that a sinner should die, and not that he should be converted from his ways and live' (Ezech. xviii. 23), and so, doing penance, should return to the grace of his Creator? And how merciful He is to the sinful soul He declares by another prophet, when He implores it, even after the sin committed, to turn again and find mercy, saying, Thou hast prostituted thyself to many lovers' (Jer. iii. 1); that is to say, thou, who hadst pledged thy faith to Me in baptism, hast stained and desecrated thy conjugal fidelity with many lovers; yet do penance and re turn to Me, and I will receive thee. Let no sinner, then, lose heart when, after having been defiled with many lovers, his soul is received again; for the Fountain of Mercy, Jesus Christ, is exhausted by the iniquities of none, polluted by the crimes of none; but, always pure and always full to over flowing with grace and sweetness, receives all who return to Him, weak though they be, sinful though they be, and whatever be the sins that have defiled them. And that all sinners, and all unjust, may be sure that they receive forgiveness of their sins, if they do really strive to put away their sins and do penance, He, the Fountain of Mercy, has suffered the very same Flesh which, as I have said, He assumed in their behalf, to be crucified; that those who were dead in sins, and could by no other means return to life again unless redeemed by the price of His Blood, might not despair at all when they should see what price has been offered for their sins.

[§ 28. The sinner's contemplation of himself.] When, then, I contemplate the so great compassion 06 my Lord Jesus Christ, and see that, although so many sinners and unjust run to the Fountain of Mercy, none are shut out, but all are welcomed, am I alone to give up hope? am I alone to fear that He who washes others clean cannot wash away my sins? I know, I know assuredly, and I truly believe, that He who cleanses others is able to cleanse me also, and, if He will, for He is most mighty, to remit me all my sins. Still, however, there are great differences between one sinner and another; between, that is to say, him who sins more grievously, and him who sins less. And I, contemplating in this respect the greatness of my sins and the deep dye of the iniquities that my soul has been stained withal, see clearly that I am not in like case with other sinners, but that I am sinner more than any other sinner, and far beyond all other sinners. For many have sinned, and then desisted; some, although they have often sinned, have yet at some time set a limit to their evil courses; others, again, even if they have done many evil deeds, have not failed also to do many good, and have thus merited either that those evil deeds should be remitted altogether, or else have gained that even the pains of hell should be more tolerable for them. But I, poor I, sinful and wretched above all sinful and all wretched mortals, understanding well and knowing well to what dire perdition my sin and the fascination of sin was leading me, have never cared to desist from sins and evil deeds, but have ever aggravated old sins by new, and thus all wittingly and wilfully have plunged myself, wretch that I am, into the perdition of sin; and, but that the infinite goodness of my Lord still bore with me, long, long ago must I have been devoured by hell itself. I then, after living as I have lived, after committing so great enormities and involving myself in so great iniquities, how shall I dare to fly to the Fountain of Mercy in the company of others, sinners, it is true, but sinners who have not done so great ill , for fear lest by reason of the foulness of my crimes He who has washed others whose foulness is more tolerable should refuse to wash me? Help me therefore, O Lord Jesus Christ, help Thy creature, overwhelmed though I be by a multitude of sins; but rather, seeing in me Thine own creation, help me lest I despair; for, as we do believe, no load of sins can be so enormous in guilt as to conquer Thee, if only the sinner despair not of Thy mercy.

[§ 29. The sinner's prayer to Jesus Christ.] Suffer me therefore, O Lord Jesus Christ, to gaze on Thy unspeakable mercy, and to tell abroad Thy sweetness and goodness towards the sinful and the wretched. I have said it already, but O, it delights me much, whenever fit occasion offers, to make remembrance of Thy sweetness and Thy grace to sinners, and to say how great they are. For, out of love for sinners and for their redemption--not merely sinners who are sinners more or less, but sinners who are sinful beyond measure, if only they repent--Thou earnest down from the Bosom of the Father, Thou didst enter the Virgin's womb, didst take true flesh of her, and living in the world didst call all sinners to penance, at last didst endure the gibbet of the Cross for them, and dying thus according to the flesh, didst restore to them the life which by their sin they had justly lost. Therefore, when I consider the evil deeds that I have done, I am sure that I shall be lost, if Thou shouldest please to judge me according to my deserts; but, when I consider that death of Thine which Thou didst undergo for the redemption of sinners, I do not despair of Thy mercy. Why; the thief who for his sins was crucified by Thy side lived on in sin, to the very passing away of his soul in death; and yet, in the very hour of his dissolution, because he confessed his faults and proclaimed his guilt, found mercy and was that very day with Thee in Paradise. And I, beholding Thee, as I do, dead for the redemption of sinners, Thy Hands and Thy Feet fastened by the nails, Thy Side opened by the soldier's lance, the river of Blood and Water flowing from that dear Side of Thine, am I to despair? One thing, and one thing only, dost Thou desire; that is, that we re pent of our wickednesses, and endeavour to amend as best we may. If we do this, we are safe; for if our last day finds us thus--since we have the instance of the thief who thus in his last hour merited to be saved--confiding in the unspeakable mercy of our Lord Jesus Christ, we may have little or no fear of the accusation of the enemy. Having, therefore, before our eyes the price of our redemption, the Death, that is to say, of our Redeemer, and His Blood which was shed for us; having, besides, the example of the thief and of many who, having been entangled in many and great sins, have been mercifully forgiven by Him, the Fountain of Mercy, Jesus Christ, let us not despair, but fly, sure of the remission of our sins, to Him the Fountain of Mercy, in whom we see and know that so many and so great sinners have been washed clean; and let us be sure that we in like manner shall be cleansed by the same Fountain of Mercy, if we abstain from our wickednesses and our sins, and, as far as we can, have a care to do what is right. But, to abstain from evil and do good, is what we cannot compass by our own strength and without His help. Let us, therefore, implore His unspeakable compassion, whose care it was to create us when we were not, that He would grant us thus in this life, before we go forth hence, to amend our faults; that, this life ended, we may have strength to travel home to Him in a straight unfettered flight, and so may dwell with Him in everlasting glory, joined with the angelic choirs who now enjoy it, rejoicing in unending bliss.

SEVENTH MEDITATION

[§ 30.] I. Of the changefulness of all that is in the world. Nothing is more certain than death, nothing more uncertain than the hour of death. Let us then reflect how short our life is, how slippery our path; how certain our death, how uncertain the hour of our death. Let us consider what bitternesses are mixed up with whatever of sweet or pleasant chances to allure us if we come within its reach in the course of our life's journey. O, how deceitful and how false, how changeful and how fugitive, is all the offspring of this world's love, all the pretence of transitory grace and beauty, all the promise of carnal pleasure! And let us also ponder well the sweetness and loveliness, the serenity and calm, of our own heavenly home; let us think well whence it is that we have fallen and where we lie, what we have lost and what found, that so we may learn from either consideration what good need we have to mourn and lament in this our banishment. It is for this reason that Solomon declares, He that addeth knowledge addeth also labour' (Eccles. i. 18); for the more thoroughly a man understands what are his soul's maladies, the more abundant food has he for sighs and grief. Thus, in truth, meditation engenders knowledge, knowledge invites to compunction, compunction urges to devotion, and devotion leads to prayer. By habits of unremitting meditation man is so enlightened as to know himself, whilst in the practice of compunction his heart is touched with an intimate sorrow from the contemplation of its ills.

[§ 31.] II. Of the manifold blessings of Almighty God. Poor me, how ardently ought I to love my Lord for creating me when I was not, and for redeeming me when I was lost. I was not, and He made me out of nothing; nor did He make me one amongst His many creatures that are de void of reason, as a tree, a bird, or one of the brute creation; but He willed that I should be a man, and endowed me with the gifts of life, sensation, and discourse of reason. I was lost, and to save me He stooped to my dying lot; immortal, He assumed mortality, endured suffering, vanquished death, and thus restored me to my first estate. Thus, thus have His grace and mercy always prevented me, and from many dangers He my deliverer has set me free. When I was going astray He led me back; when I knew nothing He taught me; when I sinned He chastened me; in my griefs He consoled me; in my despair He comforted; when I was fallen He raised me up; when I stood He held me; when I moved He guided me; when I came to Him He welcomed and received me. All this, and very much besides, has my Lord Jesus Christ done for me; and sweet will be the task of giving Him in return unceasing thanks for all, so may I for all His benefits be able to love and praise Him evermore. I have nothing that I can offer Him for all these things, except only that I love Him with all my heart; and there is no better and no fitter offering than what is given out of love.

[§ 32.] III. Here the sinner chides himself for his ingratitude. Alas, alas, alas, Lord God, is it so that I dare to come, that I dare to present myself in the presence of Thy saints; I of all men the most wretched and most sad; I that am so ungrateful for so many and so great blessings; I that have so shamelessly and so gracelessly abused Thy gifts; I that have not blushed out of those very gifts to make weapons wherewith to fight against Thee, and that so often and so long; I that have not blushed, so often and so long, though the recipient of Thy bounty, to fight on the devil's side against Thee, my King; I that have dared to turn Thy very gifts into arms in the devil's service; I that have presumed so infamously to misuse my very self, and dared to hire myself as a slave to the devil, and make my members his; and in those very members do battle against Thee, my Creator, against Thee, .Thou that didst make them and didst give them me.

Am I not he, O Lord my God, that has so often put himself as a sharp sword in the hands of the graceless fiend for the devouring of souls? O, how often have I set myself in array against Thee to compass my neighbour's death! And as often as I have aimed the arrows of detraction or of flattery at other men, so often have I turned it into a bow of falsehood. O most merciful, O sweetest Father, I cannot count the times that I have infamously misused my bodily members, so giving arms to the devil, and fighting against Thee, for all that Thou art utmost gentleness and goodness.

[§ 33.] IV. An acknowledgment of sin. I am the maddest of all madmen, who, created by Thee out of nothing, chosen out of the mass of sin and perdition to be a child of Thy. grace, adopted by Thee to be a joint-heir of Thy dearest and only- begotten Son Jesus Christ our Lord and God, designed for the honours and the glories of Thy Kingdom, and filled with abundance of undeserved grace, yet forgot all this Thy lavish bounty, even though he saw full well that these so great blessings had been given him by Thee. Yes, indeed, I have spurned the honours of Thy heavenly kingdom, disdained Thy glory, and reduced myself to the condition of a bastard and degenerate child, and given myself over to the devil, to be dragged at his will over the dung hills of luxury and through the thorny brakes of avarice, and to be beaten on the rocks by the waves and breakers of pride. I am the blind trader, who bartered away the priceless riches of the talents Thou gavest him, bartered them away, poor wretch, for want, for nakedness, for unending sighs; yes, I have ex changed peace the most delightsome and most joyous for thorns and a dunghill, that is to say, for riches and luxury; and pawned everlasting light for everlasting darkness, endless joys for endless griefs, eternal glory for eternal shame, and a throne in Thy kingdom for thraldom to devils.

I am that weakest of the sons of men who exposed himself as a butt for the arrow; for I have set myself to be pierced by the shafts of sin and torn from head to foot with wounds.

I am the mortal that, cast forth as a corpse to be torn and dragged to pieces by dogs of hell and all filthy carrion birds, cast forth from Thy holy city, the city of Thy holy ones, Thy friends, from the holy gladsome society of the blessed spirits of heaven, have given myself up to be consumed by vices as if by worms. O, how loathsome do I show in Thy holy eyes; stained and befouled with hideous noisome filth of luxury, scorched with fire of anger and avarice, my limbs infested with worms of hatred and envy, inflated and swollen by pride, from head to foot a mass of ulcers, scars, and wounds, stamped and scored with so many and so great sins, the lines and characters of diabolical foulness. I know, O merciful Lord, that Thou mayest deservedly and very justly say that I am none of Thine, and refuse to own in such a thing as I am, I will not say Thy child, but even Thy creation. For this hideous monstrous spectacle of all sorts of foulness is not Thy creation and re-creation; this hateful thing is no just image and similitude of Thee. It was quite an other creation that Thou madest me. Ah me! This likeness to the devil in all his foulness shows me hitherto to have been a child of the devil, an heir of the torments that await the unbelieving. Such, such is the exchange and the barter that I have made, fool, fool, blind fool that I have been, of pawning the glory and the dignity of bearing Thy likeness for most hateful and most vile deformity.

[§ 34. The sinner's review of himself.] O holy Father, Thou didst not therefore intrust those precious talents of Thine to me, as to have me yield Thee for usury so hateful an offence. Thou didst not therefore shed so many and so great benefits upon me, that Thou shouldest reap no better fruit from the seed sown than worthless weeds and thorns and thistles. Thou didst not therefore fill me and enrich me with so many and so great benefits, that I should turn them into weapons against Thee my God. It was not the design of Thy lovingkindness to give me arms against Thyself, nor to increase the devil's power by arms of Thy giving. And now behold me. See, see, I am stricken with all these wounds, these fearful wounds, yet I do not suffer. Ah, surely, I am blind; for with all their foulnesses and this utter nakedness, yet I am not ashamed.

Yes, yes indeed; I am senseless and dull of heart, not to grieve over the so many and the so sad losses that I have suffered; not even to have spirit left in me to bewail the death that I am dying. Yes, yes indeed; my heart must be of stone, that I am so hardened as not even now and then upon occasion to dread the eternal torments that overhang me. Yes, yes indeed; this heart is a rock of ice, for all the fires of my all-pitiful Father's love and His love's blessings do not avail to warm it. Yes, yes indeed; I take shame to myself and chide myself, for the trumpet-cry of preaching and the thunders of Thy threatenings are alike in effectual to arouse me.

Where is the piercing grief of which they tell, the grief of compunction, with which to crush and fling away all this hell-inspired hardness, and annihilate all the stone, the stubbornness, the rebellion? Where, my God, is the shame that should cover me with confusion before Thine eyes and the eyes of all the whole court of heaven? Where is the dread of Thy vengeance, that should make me tremble through and through before Thee? Where is the love, and the desire of recovering Thy peace and love and grace, that ought to burn within me? Where are the torrents of tears with which I should wash away my stains and my defilements from before Thee? Where is the prayerful devotion by which I should strive to appease and propitiate Thee? Whither shall I turn, O tender and com passionate Father, having, as I have, nothing worthy of Thy regard that I can offer to Thy majesty? Whither shall I fly, most merciful Father, I that am empty of all good; nay, that stand displayed full of all evil; beneath the gaze of Thy saints and the holy armies of Thy celestial hosts?

[§ 35. The sinner's cry to God.] I know, O Lord God, Thou Ruler of my life, that every best gift and every perfect gift is from above, coming down from the Father and Fountain of lights (St. James i. 16). I know that I can offer no acceptable pleasing thing to Thee, unless I have first drawn it from the Fountain of Thy goodness: and this only if Thou enlighten and if Thou teach me. I know that this earnest of Thy mercy must go before all effort of mine. I know, dearest Father, that if I cannot pilfer or filch away Thy good things from Thee, equally impossible is it for me, by any merits of mine, to procure the means where by to return to Thee and please Thee. For what due can merits of mine procure me but the punishment of eternal death? I know that it rests with Thy good pleasure whether Thou destroy me, ac cording to the multitude of my evil deeds, my offences, my neglects, and my omissions; or re make me, and make me acceptable to Thee after the inestimable riches of Thy mercy; for Thou, the sole maker of Thy creature, canst alone re make it. Now do I fly to Thee, O merciful Father, knowing that Thou art my only refuge from Thyself. Who can deliver me from Thy Hands but Thou only? Thy mercy can deliver me--the mercy which I have not only demerited but resisted and re belled against--can deliver me from Thy all-just anger, which I have so wretchedly and so gratuitously provoked. Deign, therefore, to receive me, O Lord, now that I return to Thee. Turn away, I pray Thee, Thy all-holy eyes from my foulnesses and my ingratitudes; and bend them on Thyself, from whom none ever asks forgiveness without hope of winning it. In Thyself wilt Thou find at once the source and the justification of any mercy Thou mayest show, according to the abundance of Thy sweetness and the immensity of Thy mercy. Do not, I pray Thee, look upon me; for in me Thou wilt find nothing but what well deserves Thy wrath, or is all worthy of eternal death. Then turn away Thy holy eyes, O Lord, from the sight of all that is so base and vile in me; the which, if I could see and scan them in Thy clear and blazing light, for very horror I could not endure it, but should abhor and shun my very self. Turn, turn away from my noisome foulness, and turn Thee to Thyself. I know, O Lord of mercy, that Thy holy eyes are pure, and cannot look upon horrible deformity, unless Thou give me goodness wherewithal to please Thee. I know that all Thy heavenly court turn away their eyes and shut their ears, unable to endure my hateful of fences. But Thou, O merciful Father, turn, turn to that Fountain of Mercy, whose mercy knows no measure and no end, and so look upon me Thy creature with merciful and tender regard. I am Thy creature, O Lord, and the work of Thy hands.

Remake, therefore, I beseech Thee, what Thou, didst make in me, and destroy what I have done in myself against Thy commandments. Destroy, I mean, whatever Thou hatest in me, and what ever not Thou hast made, but I, poor I. Remake and recreate what Thou didst create and make; for this is Thine, O Lord my God; and to hate what is Thine is an impossible reach of hatred, for Thou hatest none of the things which Thou hast made' (Wisdom xi. 25). Destroy in me that which is mine, that, in short, which Thou hast not made; that is to say, all my baseness and vileness; but destroy not me. Destroy it, O merciful, com passionate Lord, for Thou hatest it; and that I am beginning to hate it, is Thy good gift.

EIGHTH MEDITATION

THE PENITENT'S ADDRESS TO GOD HIS FATHER.

[36. A prayer for mercy and help.] O heavenly Father, look, I beseech Thee, upon the everflowing fountain of Thy compassion, which, as a flood of cleansing, a flood precious beyond all price, and full of life, gushed from Thy dearest and only-begotten Son for the cleansing of the world; by the death of Whom Thy goodness has been even pleased to give us life, and also to wash us with His Blood. Nay more; Thou hast consigned Thy dearest Son to men as a shield of Thy good-will a shield wherewith to shelter themselves from Thy wrath; He receiving in Himself the death they fear, He presented as a shield to Thy justice and Thy all-just anger. Nor only so; it pleased Thy mercy that not only should He bear the brunt of Thy wrath, but endure our death as well. 'Twas so indeed; Thy Son, Thine Only-begotten, has alone borne our death.

Remember, O Lord, Thy bowels of compassion, and Thy mercies that are from the beginning of the world' (Ps. xxiv. 6), and stretch out Thy hand to Thy creature that stretches forth to Thee. Help the weakness of him that struggles after Thee. Draw me; for Thou knowest that I cannot come to Thee, except Thou, the Father, draw me with the cords of love and desire. Make me a servant acceptable and pleasing unto Thee; for Thou knowest that I cannot please Thee else. Give me, I pray Thee, those holy gifts with which alone to please Thee, Thou that givest good gifts to them that ask Thee. Grant, I pray Thee, that my sole love and sole desire may be Thyself; my sole love and only fear, Thyself. Take me wholly for Thine own, Thou who knowest that to Thee I owe all that I am, all that I have, all that I know, and all my powers. Convert me wholly to Thy praise and glory, I that owe myself wholly to Thy praise. Deliver not, I pray Thee, Thy creature to Thy enemies; keep me for Thyself, whose alone I am entirely; and perfect in every part what Thou hast begun, and confirm what Thou hast wrought.

Hear my prayer, I beseech Thee, Thou who givest and inspirest it even ere I thought to call to Thee. Look upon Thy suppliant, Thou Who when I had a mind to pray didst even then deign to look upon me. Not in vain, O Lord of mercy, didst Thou deign to inspire that my prayer, not for nothing didst Thou give it me. Nay, for this very end didst Thou deign to give it, that Thou mightest listen to me; for this didst Thou grant it to me, that I might implore Thee to have mercy on me a sinner. So thus having given me an earnest of Thy mercy, give me the rest. Rescue me, O Lord my God, and snatch me out of the hands of my enemies; for they too are Thine, they are the subjects of Thy almighty power; and they hate no thing of good works in me except what Thou hast given me. There is nothing in me that they hate, but only that I love Thee. And they scheme with all their endeavours, with all their might, with all their craft, to prevent my loving Thee, glorifying Thee, and ever seeking Thee. Therefore let not the enemies of Thy glory be too strong for me; but let them be the more confounded as they see that I, bent on praising Thee and glorifying Thee, am seeking with all best endeavours that peace and glory of Thine, which they are intent upon diminishing. O Lord, let not, I beseech Thee, their so unholy and execrable design concerning me, nay, against me, be brought to pass; but enlarge Thou my soul, O Lord, for telling forth Thy praise and heralding Thy glory, that I may henceforth live altogether according to Thy great glory, and that my whole life may glorify Thee; and do Thou by my example invite and incite many of Thy predestined to glorify Thee. Let the presence of Thy light, and the sweetness of Thy glory, a glory which they can not bear, drive away from me the vile, unclean, and hateful spirits of darkness. O break my chains asunder, and take me out of durance, out of the horrible, black, and gloomy prison, out of the lake of misery and the mire of dregs, out of the abyss of death and darkness; and lead me forth into liberty and Thy marvellous light.

Enlighten me with Thy saving faith; gladden and strengthen me with Thy joyful and never-faltering hope; quicken me with Thy mighty and all-holy love. Subdue and humble me, and guard me with Thy strongest, securest, and most invincible fear. Fill me with wholesome shame from Thy all-lovely and all-glorious Self. And whensoever I present anything before Thine eyes that may offend them, break me, chastise me with pain greater than a woman's, and medicine me, after Thine own sweet fashion, with most efficacious compunction from Thyself, that I go not out from Thy mercy's presence empty and confounded; but obtain whatsoever by Thy bidding, by Thy gift, by Thy inspiration, I may ask, and whatsoever Thou hast promised unto them that ask. Let me find, O compassionate and merciful Lord, that not in vain do men fly for refuge to Thy mercy; that

Thou art very close to all who seek Thee, helping them to find Thee; and that I can never faint or fail so long as I am with Thee, the Fountain of Compassion, O Thou who hast snatched me from the pit, and lavished on me Thou knowest how much, Thou knowest what. Ay, with what uneffort of omnipotence, of wisdom, and of goodness, wherewith Thou saidst and all things were made, with a like uneffort of compassion Thou canst speak, and all my deformities can be corrected and restored to sightliness.

[§ 37. The penitent's hope in the Divine mercy.] And now, almighty and merciful Father, behold I have enumerated so many and so great Thy benefits which I have received from Thee; I have recounted the ills, so many and so great, which I have repaid Thee for Thy goodness. O wretched I, O thankless I, that for all so many and so great ills await and overhang me, yet appear before Thee with a heart obdurate and stolid, and dead and cold; and still am not ashamed. Detected in misdeeds so many and grievous, with no better prospect in the future than a gibbet in hell, still I am neither palsied with fright, nor tortured with grief, nor confounded with shame: no, nor set on fire with love of Thy so gentle and so long-forbearing goodness. What, art Thou waiting, dearest Father, and delaying to look on me and pity me, until, according to the measure of Thy mercy, I shall have become fit to appear in Thy Presence, and present in Thy Presence some thing fit to ask of Thee, and say something fit for Thee to listen to? See, see, it is a corpse that I have brought Thee; a corpse swarming with worms, and three days dead, is what comes to Thee, Thou Giver of life. See, see; what I present to Thy almighty mercy is one blind, to be illuminated; one sick, to be made whole; one involved in, O how many and how great debts, to be set free; stark-naked and poverty-stricken, to be enriched. For easy it is to Thee to enrich a beggar in a moment.

Nor can I otherwise, most clement God, than offer Thee myself, just as I am; show Thee my death and wounds, my nakedness and poverty, and my debts, for which I fear the dungeon of everlasting death. Do Thou, then, show me Thine Eyes of mercy; if, indeed, Thou canst be turned and canst forgive, and canst pour upon me of Thy grace and bliss. For turn myself to Thee I can not; I am wounded with too many and too deep wounds; I am borne down by sicknesses and even death, and am become altogether helpless. But do Thou, O merciful Father, convert me, and I shall be converted to Thee. Convert me to Thee, O Lord (Lam. v. 21), and bruise and crush my heart, and implant in me the sensibilities of a quickening grief. For there is no fountain of blessings besides Thee; there is none from whom to receive love and fear, and grief and shame, wherewith to appear in Thy sight and be found worthy of Thy mercy, unless Thou, from the vast reservoir of Thy mercy, pour out grace on me, so all unworthy of Thy grace. O Lord, if Thou give me this, I shall be happy. If Thou vouch safe to chastise my offences and my crimes ac cording to Thy judgment and thy justice, O happy I; not so, if Thou correct me in Thy fury [Jer. x. 24], the fury which in the end overtakes and seizes all who rebel against and dare Thy mercy.

And this, O merciful Father, is Thy judgment and Thy justice; even this, that fear, love, shame, and grief work in the hearts of all who truly re pent and return to Thy goodness, that they may gain Thy mercy. Pierce, then, this thief with Thy holy fear, and burn this rebel with the fire of Thy love and charity; pierce, O Lord, this malefactor with life-giving and most wholesome sorrow from Thee; confuse this unblushing sinner with shame from thy glorious Self; nail, nail this miscreant to his cross of penal anguish, and let that anguish conciliate Thy mercy. Make me hunger for Thee with all my heart, and thirst for Thee with all my bowels; make me serve only Thee with all my inward parts, and with all my energies pursue what is well-pleasing in Thy sight. And so to Thee, with Jesus Christ, Thine only-begotten Son and our Lord, and with the Holy Ghost, the Paraclete, Thy most holy Gift, be all honour and glory for ever and ever. Amen.

NINTH MEDITATION

OF THE HUMANITY OF CHRIST.

[§ 38. The glories and the condescension of our Lord Jesus Christ.] Let Jesus of Nazareth, who, though innocent, was condemned by the Jews and fastened to the cross by the Gentiles, be worshipped by us Christians with the honours due to Him as God. Let us who are Christ's render to our Saviour's griefs the homage of trembling adoration, of loving embrace, and of a courageous following; for this is meet, honourable, and available to salvation. For they are the potent instruments wherewith the almighty power and inscrutable wisdom of God wrought out, and even now works out, the restoration of the world. Christ the Lord was made a little less than the angels, that we might be made equal unto the angels; and who would not humble himself for the sake of Christ? Christ the Lord was crucified for our sins, and has sweetened to His lovers all the bitters of the Cross. He died, and dying destroyed death, that we might live through Him; and who would not love Christ the Lord? who would not suffer for Christ? Christ through the shame of the Cross has passed into the brightness of supremest glory, and for His reverence (Heb. v. 7) all power in heaven and in earth has been given to Him by God the Father, that all the angels of God may adore Him, and that in His Name every knee may bow of those that are in heaven, and in earth, and in hell (Phil, ii. 10).

Where then, O Christian, is thy boasting, if it be not in the Name of thy crucified Lord, Jesus Christ; in the Name which is above every name, the Name in which He who is blessed on earth shall be blessed in heaven? O boast in His holy Name, ye children of redemption; pay honour to your Saviour, who has done great things in us, and magnify His Name with me, saying, We adore Thee, O Christ, King of Israel, Prince of the kings of the earth, Light of the Gentiles, Lord of hosts, most mighty virtue of the omnipotent God. We adore Thee, O priceless price of our redemption, our peace-offering, who alone, by the wonderful sweetness of Thy odour, hast inclined Thy Father who dwells in heaven to regard our lowliness, and hast Thyself alone propitiated Him. O Christ, we speak abroad Thy mercies, we tell, and tire not in telling, of the memory of Thy sweetness; to Thee, O Christ, we offer the sacrifice of praise for the abundance which Thou hast shown us of Thy goodness, us, wicked seed that we are and ungracious children.'

For when as yet we were Thine enemies, O Lord, and ancient death held sway over all flesh--a sway to which the whole seed of Adam was subject by the necessary law and condition of their primal guilt--Thou wast mindful of Thy all-abounding mercy, and didst look forth from Thy lofty dwelling on this our valley of misery and tears. Thou didst see, O Lord, the affliction of Thy people, and, touched to the heart with charity and sweetness, didst apply Thyself to think thoughts of peace and redemption for us. And although Thou wast the Son of God, true God co-eternal and consubstantial with God the Father and the Holy Ghost, inhabiting the inaccessible light' (1 Tim. vi. 16), and upholding all things by the word of Thy power' (Heb. i. 3), Thou didst not disdain to lower Thy majesty to this prison of our mortality, there to taste and swallow up our misery and restore us to glory. It was too little for Thy charity to destine cherubim or seraphim, or any one of the angelic choirs, to consummate the work of our salvation. Thou didst condescend to come to us in Thy own Person by the will of the Father, of whose abounding charity we have in Thee made proof. Thou earnest, I say, not by a local change, but by exhibition of Thy Person to us in the flesh. Thou didst stoop from the royal throne of Thy sublime glory into a humble maiden and abject in her own sight, a maiden sealed by the early vow of virginal chastity. In whose sacred womb the unspeakable power of the Holy Ghost caused Thee to be conceived, and thence to be born in the true nature of our humanity, in such wise that the majesty of the Godhead should not be violated in Thyself, nor the virginal integrity of Thy Mother sullied by the occasion of Thy birth.

[§ 39. The Nativity of Christ, and its sanctification of poverty.] O loveable, O admirable condescension! God of boundless glory, Thou didst not disdain to be made a contemptible worm. Lord of all things, Thou didst appear as a slave among slaves. It seemed too little to Thee to be our Father; Thou didst deign, O Lord, to be our Brother also. Nay, more; Thou, Thou the Lord of all things, who hadst need of nothing, didst not refuse, even at the very outset of Thy human life, to taste to the full the inconveniences of most abject poverty. For, as the Scripture says, there was no room for Thee in the inn (St. Luke ii. 7) when Thou wast about to be brought forth, nor hadst Thou cradle to receive Thy frail and delicate frame; but Thou, Thou who boldest the earth in the palm of Thy Hand, wast laid, wrapt in rags, in the vile manger of a filthy cattle-shed; and Thy Mother shared with brute beasts a stall for her hospice. Be comforted, be comforted, you that are nurtured in filth and want, for your God is with you in your poverty. He does not lie cradled in splendour and luxury; no, nor is He found in the domains of those whose life is a life of ease. Why, O rich man, do you boast any longer I why do you boast, O thing of clay, as; you lie lolling in your couch of luxury and colour, while He, the King of kings, has preferred to dignify the pauper's bed of straw by lying on it? Why do you loathe hard beds, while He, the frail Baby-God, in whose Hand all things are, has chosen for His pallet the hard straw where cattle lie, in preference to your cover lets of silk and pillows of down?

But even this Thy tender infancy, O Christ, was not safe from persecutors' swords. Thou wast still hanging a sucking-child at Thy Mother's breast when an angel appeared in sleep to Joseph, saying, Arise, and take the child and his mother, and fly into Egypt, and be there until I shall tell thee; for it will come to pass that Herod will seek the child, to destroy him' (St. Matt. ii. 13). Thus even then, good Jesus, didst Thou begin to suffer. Nay, not only didst Thou endure in Thine own Person that persecution of Thine infancy, but even death in the person of Thy little ones, thousands and thousands of whom were slaughtered by the ruthless Herod at their mothers' breasts for Thy sake.

[§ 40. The hidden life and ministry of our Lord.] And on finishing Thy course of early boy hood Thou didst bequeath us an example how to learn the truth with humility. For although Thou wast the Lord of all knowledge (1 Kings ii. 3) and the Very Personal Wisdom of God the Father, yet didst Thou sit--not with the council of vanity (Ps. xxv. 4)--but in the midst of the doctors, asking them questions and listening to them. And furthermore, Thou gavest us an instance of obedience in living humbly subject to the rule of pa rents, for all that Thou wast the Master of the world.

And when Thou didst attain the strength of riper age, and wast ready to lay to Thy hand for mighty deeds, then Thou didst issue forth for the saving of Thy people, like a giant strong to run the race of our sad estate (Ps. xviii. 6); and first of all, to be made in all things like Thy brethren, Thou didst--as though Thou wert indeed a sinner approach--Thy servant who baptized sinners with the baptism of penance, and didst even implore him to baptize Thee, Thee, innocent

59

Lamb of God, whom slightest taint of sin had never stained. Thou wast baptized, not to sanctify Thyself by the waters, but to sanctify the waters by Thyself, that so through them we might be sanctified by Thee. And then Thou wentest forth in the Spirit of power, fresh from the baptismal wave, into the desert, that a pattern of the solitary life also might not be wanting in Thy Person. Loneliness, forty days' fast, the sharp tooth of hunger, temptations from the deceiver-spirit,--all were borne by Thee with even mind, that thus all might by Thy working be made bearable to us. This done, Thou then earnest to the sheep that had been lost of the house of Israel (St. Matt. x. 6), lifting on high the torch of the Divine word for the illumination of the world; and, preaching the kingdom of God to all men, didst become the source of eternal salvation to all that obey, and confirm Thy preaching by signs following, and show forth the power of Thy Godhead to all that were in evil case; freely displaying to all all things that made for their salvation, that so Thou mightest gain all. But their foolish heart, O Lord, was darkened (Rom. i. 21), and they cast Thy words behind them (Ps. xlix. 17), and heeded not all the wonders that Thou didst work among them; except some few great heroic souls, whom Thou didst choose out from the contemptible and base things of the world, that by them Thou mightest gloriously bring to naught the strong and lofty (1 Cor. i. 27, 28). But not alone were men unthankful to Thee for Thy all-gratuitous benefits; they assailed Thee with insults, O Lord of all lords, and did unto Thee what soever they had a mind (St. Matt. xvii. 12). For when Thou didst among them works of God none else did, what said they? This man is not of God' (St. John ix. 16); He casteth out devils by Beelzebub the prince of devils' (St. Luke xi. 15); He hath a devil' (St. Matt. xi. 18); He seduces the people;' He is a glutton and a winebibber, a friend of publicans and sinners' (St. Matt. xi. 19).

[§ 41. The meekness and humility of Christ.] Why, then, weep, O man of God, why sigh for sorrow when injurious words are heaped upon you? Do you not hear what insults were levelled, and all for your sake, at your Lord and God? If they have called the good man of the house Beelzebub, how much more them of his household?' (St. Matt. x. 25.) Ah, good Jesus, they assailed Thee with these and such-like blasphemies, and sometimes even hurled stones at Thee; yet Thou didst bear all patiently, and wast made before them as a man that heareth not, and that hath no reproofs in his mouth (Ps. xxxvii. 15). At last they bargained with a disciple of Thine, the son of perdition, for Thy just blood, for thirty pieces of silver (St. Matt. xxvii. 9), that they might yield Thy soul to death without a cause. Nor was the villany of Thy all-foredone betrayer unknown to Thee, even when Thou didst deign with Thy all holy Hands to touch, to wash, to wipe those cursed feet, so swift for the shedding of Thy Blood.

And yet you still walk with outstretched neck, O dust and earth; conceit still lifts you up above your proper self, and impatience of control still urges you immoderately on! See, see thy Teacher of humility and lowliness, see thy Lord Jesus Christ, see the Creator of the universal world, see the dread Judge of living and dead kneeling upon His knees at the feet of a man, and that man His betrayer; and learn that He is meek and humble of heart' (St. Matt. xi. 29), and be confounded for your pride, and blush for shame at your peevishness.

And it was one sign more of Thy gentleness, Lord Jesus, that refusing openly to detect and confound the traitor in presence of his brethren, Thou didst give a kind hint, and bid him hasten what was in preparation. And yet for all this his madness was not diverted from Thee; but he went out, and busied himself about his repeated villany. How art thou fallen from heaven, O Lucifer! who didst rise in the morning' (Is. xiv. 12) in the delights of paradise; for thou wast glorious to behold, companion of the citizens of heaven, and guest of the Word Divine; thou that wast brought up in scarlet (Lam. iv. 5), hast thou indeed embraced the dung?

Then was Thy household, O Lord, glorified so as to be like the company of the angels; then, then at last was that happy society satisfied with the outpoured draughts of the Divine word that is sued from Thy mouth. For that polluted one had been dismissed whom Thou knewest to be unfit for the inpouring of that clear limpid stream.

[§ 42. The agony and the betrayal.] When, however, the maundy of a Saviour's charity and patience had been given, and the kingdom of Thy Father consigned to Thy brethren, Thou didst retire with them to the place known to the traitor, knowing all the things that were about to come upon Thee, and then and there didst not shrink from pouring into Thy brethren's ear that sorrow of soul which at the prospect of Thy impending Passion, like all those sufferings themselves when present to Thee, Thou didst undergo with perfect willingness: My soul is sorrowful even unto death' (St. Matt. xxvi. 38). And kneeling down Thou didst fall on Thy face, praying in an agony, and saying, Abba, Father! My Father, if it be possible, let this chalice pass from Me' (ib. 39). And the anguish of Thy sorrowing Heart was betrayed by that sweat of blood which, what time Thou prayedst, rolled down in drops to the ground from Thy all-sacred Flesh. O Lord, and Lord of lords, Christ Jesus, why this so racking grief of soul, why this torture with such a rain of sweat, why this tortured supplication? For didst Thou not offer an entirely willing sacrifice to the Father, enduring nothing whatever without Thy will's consent? Yes, Lord; yes indeed. But we believe that Thou didst take upon Thee this also for the consolation of Thy weak members, lest any of us should despair if the weak flesh murmur while yet his spirit is ready for suffering. And doubtless it was that we might have greater incentives still to love of Thee, and gratitude, that Thou didst set forth the natural weakness of the flesh by such kind of tokens as might make us learn that Thou hast verily borne our sicknesses Thyself, and didst not tread the thorny course of Thy Passion without the sense of physical pain. For that cry was the cry--as it should seem--of the flesh, not of the spirit, inasmuch as Thou didst add, The spirit indeed is willing, but the flesh weak' (St. Matt. xxvi. 41). And Thy Spirit's readiness, good Jesus, for Thy Passion Thou didst evidence clearly enough, in going forth to meet the men of blood as they drew near with the traitor, searching through the night for Thy life, with lanterns, torches, and weapons; and in shewing that it was Thou Thyself by accepting what they had received as the token from their guide in guilt. For as the murderous creature came near to Thee for the kiss of Thy Mouth, Thou didst not recoil, but didst sweetly place upon the mouth that ran over with wickedness that Mouth in which no deceit was found (Is. liii. 9).

What, O innocent Lamb of God, what hadst Thou in common with that wolf? What concord hath Christ with Belial?' (2 Cor. vi. 15.) But here again was Thy loving-kindness displayed in showing him all instances that could have served to soften the obduracy of a wicked heart; for Thou didst remind him of Thy ancient friendship in the words, Friend, whereto art thou come?' (St. Matt, xxvi. 50.) And Thou didst wish to strike a horror of his sin into that sacrilegious heart when Thou saidst to him, Judas, dost thou betray the Son of Man with a kiss?' (St. Luke xxii. 48.) For the Philistines are upon thee, Samson' (Judges xvi. 14). But they were not frightened from their intent for all that, at the very moment of Thy seizure, Thou didst strike them to the earth with Thy omnipotent arm; not in self-defence, indeed, but that man's presumption might be taught that it cannot avail aught against Thee, except by Thy allowance. And who can hear without a sigh how in that hour they laid their murderous hands on Thee, and, Thy Hands, Thy innocent Hands, good Jesus, being bound with cords, dragged Thee like a thief, Thee the gentlest Lamb, silent and unreproachful, with all insult to the slaughter? Yet even then, O Christ, the honey-comb of Thy sweetness ceased not to distil its mercy even on Thy foes; for Thou didst heal an enemy's ear, wounded by Thy disciple, and didst restrain Thy defender's zeal from striking in Thy behalf. O accursed madness, O stubborn hate, which neither the grandeur of the miracle nor the kindness of the cure availed to subdue and crush.

[§ 43. The condemnation and the crucifixion.] Then wast Thou presented before the chief-priest's council, who were enraged against Thee, and for confessing the truth, as it behoved Thee, wast condemned to death on the charge of blasphemy. Jesus, most loving Lord, what indignities hast Thou not endured from Thine own nation! Thy adorable Face, which the angels long to stare at, and all the whole heavens are filled full with joy in gazing on, and the rich among the people do entreat (Ps. xliv. 13); they stained it with spittings from pol-luted lips, they struck it with sacrilegious hands, and covered it with a veil in derision; and Thee, the Lord of the universal world, they buf-feted like a contemptible slave. And as though this were not enough, they gave Thy life over to an uncircumcised dog to be devoured, de-manding that Thou who knewest no sin shouldest be done to death by the punishment of the cross, and that a murderer should be given them (Acts iii. 3), preferring thus a wolf to the Lamb, and clay to Gold. O unworthy and O ill-starred compact! And yet the sacrilegious Pilate knew that this had been done to Thee for envy; still he withheld not his presumptuous hands from Thee, but filled Thy soul with bitterness without a cause; sent Thee off to be mocked, took Thee back again when mocked, made Thee stand naked before the eyes of Thy tormen-tors, and shrank not from tearing and gashing Thy virginal flesh with rods, laying bruises upon bruises with reiterated cruelty.

What, O Chosen Child of my Lord God, hadst Thou done to deserve such bitterness, to deserve such shame? Nothing, nothing. Un-done mortal that I am, 'tis I that was the cause of all Thy tribulation and all Thy shame; 'tis I who ate the sour grapes, and Thy teeth were numbed, for Thou hast paid what Thou tookest not away (Ps. lxviii. 5).. But the impiety of the perfidious Jews was even thus unsatisfied; for at last Thou wast turned over into the hands of uncircumcised sol-diers to be destroyed by a death of all deaths the shamefullest. Nor was it enough for them to crucify Thee, they first filled Thy soul with insults; for what says the Scripture? They gathered together unto Him all the whole band into the prætorium; and stripping Him they put a scar let cloak about Him; and platting a crown of thorns they put it upon His head, and a reed in His right hand; and, bowing the knee before Him, they mocked Him, saying, Hail, King of the Jews;' and they buffeted Him; and spitting upon Him they took the reed and struck His head. And after they had mocked Him, they took off the cloak from Him, and led Him away to crucify Him,' bearing His own Cross. And they led Him out to Golgotha, and they gave Him' myrrhed wine to drink, mingled with gall; and when He had tasted He would not drink' (St. Matt. xxvii. 27-34). Then they crucified Him, and with Him two others, one on each side, and Jesus in the midst' (St. John xix. 18). And Jesus said, Father, forgive them, for they know not what they do' (St. Luke xxiii. 33, 34). Afterward Jesus, knowing that all things were now accomplished, that the scripture might be fulfilled, said, I thirst' (St. John xix. 28). And one running and filling a sponge with vinegar, and putting it upon a reed, gave Him to drink' (St. Mark xv. 36). Therefore, when He had taken the vinegar, He said, It is consummated' (St. John xix. 30). And crying with a loud voice, He said, Father, into Thy hands I commend My spirit' (St. Luke xxiii. 46). And bowing His head, He gave up the ghost' (St. John xix. 30). Then one of the soldiers with a spear opened His side, and immediately there came out blood and water' (Ib. 34).

[§ 44. The humiliations of the Passion.] Now then, my soul, arouse thee; shake thee from the dust, and with fixed and earnest look gaze on this memorable Man, whom thou seest veritably present, as it were, by the mirror of the gospel story. Look, my soul, and tell me who, who is He? He walks in majesty and with all the bearing of a king, and yet laden with contempt like some poor slave, and covered with confusion. He walks in majesty, and His Head is encircled with a crown; but O, that crown of His is torture, and pierces at a thousand points that goodly brow of His. He is clad like a king, in purple, but O, it is all for despite, not for honour. He carries a sceptre in His Hand, but only that His sacred Head may be smitten with it. They bend the knee to earth and worship Him, they all proclaim Him King; and, see, forthwith they fly upon Him, spit upon His cheeks, beat His jaws with the palms of their hands, and rain dishonours on His royal neck. Look, look again, and see how this Man of men is hard bested, is spit upon, is spurned. He is bid den to bow His back beneath the burden of a heavy cross, and carry His own instrument of shame. Led out to the place of death He is given myrrh and gall to drink; He is lifted up upon the cross, saying as He rises, Father, forgive them, for they know not what they do' (St. Luke xxiii. 34). Who, who, and what is This that, for all He was so oppressed, opened not His mouth even once to utter word of complaint, of excuse, or threatening, or malediction, against the dogs that encompassed Him, and at last breathed on His enemies a word of benediction such as the world had never heard from its foundation. What hast thou ever seen, O my soul, more gentle, or more kind and tender, than this Man? But look, look still, pay greater heed to Him; for now He appears worthy of boundless wonder as of tenderest pity. See Him, all naked and scarred with stripes, fastened with iron nails to the cross between two thieves, and even after death wounded in the side with a lance, and pouring forth bountiful rivers of Blood from the five wounds of Hands, of Feet, of Side. Weep tears, O eyes of mine; melt, melt, my heart, with fires of compassion for that Man of love, so bruised, and crushed, and battered with griefs so dire, for all that His was a tenderness so sweet.

[§ 45. The glories of the Passion.] Hast thou seen Him in His weakness, O my soul, and pitied Him? Turn again, and see His majesty, and thou shalt wonder. For what says the Scripture? It was almost the sixth hour: and there was darkness over all the earth until the ninth hour, and the sun was darkened' (St. Luke xxiii. 44, 45). And, behold, the veil of the temple was rent in two from the top even to the bottom: and the earth quaked, and the rocks were rent: and the graves were opened, and many bodies of the saints that had slept arose' (St. Matt. xxviii. 51, 52). Who, who is this; for heaven and earth share His grief, and dying He brings the dead to life? Own Him, own Him, my soul; it is the Lord Jesus Christ, thy Saviour, the only-begotten Son of God, true God, true Man, who alone was found without spot beneath the sun. Yet see how He was reputed with the wicked' (Is. liii. 12), and we have thought Him as it were a leper' (ib. 4), despised and the most abject of men' (ib. 3); and f as a hidden untimely birth' (Job iii. 16) which is cast forth from the womb, so is He cast forth from the womb of His mother, the unhappy synagogue. He so lovely beyond the sons of men, how unsightly beyond the sons of men has He become! Ay, indeed; He was wounded for our iniquities, He was bruised for our sins' (Is. liii. 5); and is be come a holocaust of sweetest odour in Thy sight, O Father of eternal glory, to turn away Thine indignation from us, and make us sit along with Himself in heavenly places.

[§ 46. Joseph in Egypt a type of Christ.] Look down, O Lord, holy Father, from Thy sanctuary, and from Thy high and heavenly dwelling, and behold this all-holy Victim, which our great Highpriest, Thy holy Child Jesus, offers Thee for the sins of His brethren; and have mercy on the multitude of our iniquities. Lo, the voice of the Blood of Jesus our Brother cries to Thee from the Cross. For what is it, O Lord, that hangs on the Cross? Hangs, I say; for past things are as present with Thee. Own It, O Father. It is the coat of Thy Joseph, Thy Son; an evil wild beast hath devoured Him, and hath trampled on His Garment in its fury, spoiling all the beauty of this His remanent Corpse, and lo, five mournful gaping wounds are left in It. This is the Garment which Thy innocent holy Child Jesus, for the sins of His brethren, has left in the hands of the Egyptian harlot, thinking the loss of His robe a better thing than the loss of purity; and choosing rather to be despoiled of His coat of flesh and go down to the prison of death than to yield to the voice of the seductress for all the glory of the world. All these will I give Thee, if, falling down, Thou wilt adore me' (St. Matt. iv. 9); that is to say, if Thou wilt lie with the adultress. And now, O Lord and Father, we know that Thy Son is living, and He is Ruler in all the land of Egypt' (Gen. xlv. 26), even in all places of Thy dominion. For, led forth to Thy royal Throne from the prison of death and hell, shorn of mortality and with changed apparel of Flesh, He lives again in the bloom of immortal beauty, and with glory hast Thou welcomed Him. Pharaoh has been stricken down, Pharaoh the deadly foe, and by His own great might He has passed in lordly triumph into heaven. And now, behold, He appears at the right hand of Thy majesty for us, crowned with glory and honour, for He is our Brother and our Flesh' (Gen. xxxvii. 27).

Look, O Lord, on the Face of Thy Christ (Ps. lxxxiii. 10), who became obedient unto death to Thee. Let not the marks of His Wounds depart ever from Thine Eyes, but remember rather what satisfaction Thou hast received for our sins. O Lord, weigh in Thy balance the sins by which we have merited Thine anger, and the grief which Thy sinless Son has borne for us. Surely, O Lord, this grief of His will show more grievous than our sins, and cry louder to Thee to pour forth all Thy mercy on us than they can cry that Thou shouldest shut up Thy mercies in anger. O Lord, holy Father, let every tongue give thanks to Thee for the abundance of Thy mercy, which spared not the only Son of Thy Bosom, but gave Him up to die for us, that we might have so great and so faithful an Advocate before Thee in heaven.

[§ 47. Love our only possible return to Christ for His suffering.] And as for Thee, O Lord Jesus, Lord of almighty zeal, what due return, what worthy thanks, can I ever pay Thee, mortal that I am, dust and ashes, and worthless clay? For what was there that it behoved Thee to do for my salvation, and Thou hast not done it! From the sole of Thy foot to the crown of Thy head Thou didst plunge Thy whole Self in the waters of suffering, that all that is of me might be extricated from them; and so the waters came in even unto Thy soul (Ps. lxviii. 2). For Thou gavest up Thy soul to death to give back my lost soul to me; and so Thou hast bound me in a double debt, in that Thou gavest what Thou didst, and in that Thou didst freely give it up for my sake. Either way I am Thy debtor.

And yet again, since Thou hast twice given me life, once in creating, and once in redeeming; that life, surely, is the very best return that I could ever pay thee. But when I think of Thine own precious Soul so tortured, I know not what due return could be by mortal ever paid to Thee. For could I pay Thee in return for it all heaven, all earth, and all the bravery of heaven and earth, yet even so I should not attain to the measure of my obligation. Nay, the very giving Thee what I have and what I can, is in itself Thy gift. I must love Thee, I must love Thee, Lord, with all my heart, all my soul, all my mind, all my strength, and follow as best I can Thy footsteps, who didst deign to die for me. And how shall all this be done in me, unless Thou do it? O, let my soul cling to Thee; for all its strength comes from Thee.

[§ 48. The likeness of His Death and of His Resurrection.] And now, O Lord Jesus, my Redeemer, I adore Thee as very God; I believe in Thee, I hope in Thee, and I sigh after Thee with all possible desires; O, help my imperfection. I bow down my whole self before the glorious insignia of Thy Passion, wherewith Thou didst accomplish my salvation. The royal standard of Thy victorious Cross; in Thy Name, O Christ, do I adore it. The thorny diadem; the nails glistening with Thy Blood; the lance plunged into Thy sacred Side; Thy Wounds; Thy Blood; Thy Death; Thy Burial; Thy triumphant Resurrection, and Thy Glory,--O Christ, I suppliantly adore and glorify them. For the balm of life breathes forth on me from all of them. By their life-giving odour revive and raise my spirit from the death of sin. Shield me by their virtue from the crafts of Satan; and comfort me, O Lord, that the yoke of Thy commandments may be sweet to me, and that the burden of the cross which Thou biddest me carry after Thee may be light and portable to the shoulders of my soul. For what courage have I for bearing up according to Thy precepts against the so many and so manifold oppressions of the world? Are my feet like hart's feet, that I should be able to follow after Thee in Thy fleet passage through the thorns and roughnesses of Thy sufferings? But hear my voice, I pray Thee, and bend over Thy servant that sweet Cross of Thine, which is a tree of life to all that lay hold on it; and then will I run with alacrity, even as I hope to do; then will I carry after Thee without fainting and unweariedly the Cross Thine enemies have given Thee. Lay that divinest Cross, I pray Thee, on my shoulders; whose breadth is charity spreading over all creation; whose length, eternity; whose height, omnipotence; whose depth, unfathomable wisdom. And fasten my hands to it, and my feet; and clothe me from head to foot with the impress and the likeness of Thy Passion. Grant me, I implore Thee, to abstain from deeds of the flesh, which Thou hatest, and to do justice, which Thou lovest; and either way to seek Thy glory. So shall I deem my left hand to have been fastened with the nail of temperance, and my right hand with the nail of justice, to that lofty Cross of Thine. Let my mind meditate in Thy law continually, and direct its every thought to Thee continually; and so by the nail of prudence fasten Thou my right foot to the same tree of life. Let not the joyless joy of this fleeting life dissipate the senses, which should only minister to the spirit, nor yet its jocund joylessness waste and diminish the rewards of the life eternal laid up in store for me; and so shall my left foot also be nailed to the Cross by the nail of fortitude.

But, that some likeness may appear in me even to the thorns on Thy Head, let the compunction of a saving penance be impressed in my mind, and compassion for the miseries of others, and a penetrating zeal urging and pricking me to what is right in Thine eyes; and so shall I in my griefs be conformed to Thee, so shall the threefold wreath of thorn be fastened on me (Ps. xxxi. 4).

I would also have Thee put to my lips the sponge upon the reed, and make me taste the vinegar and its harshness; for I would have Thee, through Thy Scriptures, make my reason taste and see to see how like a sponge is all the hollow glory of the world, and how much more sour than vinegar is all the concupiscence of the world. So, Father, may it be brought to pass in me that the golden cup of Babylon that makes all the earth drunk (Jer. li. 7) may not seduce me with its worthless glitter, nor intoxicate me with its treacherous sweetness, as it does those who think darkness light, and light darkness, who think bitter sweet, and sweet bitter (Is. v. 20). And as to the wine mingled with myrrh, I suspect it, for Thou wouldest not drink of it; because, perhaps, it indicated the too great bitterness of Thy crucifiers.

And let Thy servant not only share Thy sufferings, let him also be made conformable to Thy life-giving death, by working this in me, that I may die after the flesh to sin, and live after the spirit to justice.

But that I may glory in bearing the perfect image of the Crucified, I pray Thee to express in me what the insatiable malice of sinners wrought in Thee even after Thou hadst died. Let Thy word wound my heart, Thy word living and effectual, more penetrating than the sharpest lance, and reaching even to the inmost parts of the soul; and let it draw forth from it, as though it were from my right side, in place of blood and water, love of Thee and love of my brethren.

And last of all, wrap my spirit in the clean linen of the first robe; [4] and in it let me rest, going in to Thee into the place of Thy wonderful tabernacle (Ps. xli. 5), and there hide me until Thy indignation pass away (Is. xxvi. 20).

But on the third day, the day of toil and the day of single glory overpast, on the first early morning of the week that shall see no end, do Thou revive me and raise me up, unworthy though I be, that in my flesh I may see Thy beauty, and be filled to the full with the joy of Thy countenance (Ps. xv. 11), O my Saviour and my God. Come, come the day, O my Saviour and my God; speed, speed the time; that what now I believe in I may then behold at last with unveiled eye; that what now I hope for and salute from afar, I may apprehend; that what now I desire with all my powers, I may clasp in my soul's embrace and rapturously greet; and be all swallowed up in Thy love's abyss, O my Saviour and my God! But now meanwhile, O thou my soul, bless thou thy Saviour; and magnify His Name, for it is holy and full of holiest delights.

[§ 49. Aspiration and prayer.] O how good and sweet Thou art, Lord Jesus, to the soul that seeks Thee, Jesus, Redeemer of the captives; Saviour of the lost; Hope of the exiles; Strength of those that labour; Repose of the anxious spirit; dear Solace and sweet Refreshment of the tearful soul that runs toiling after Thee; Crown of them that conquer; sole Reward and only Joy of the citizens above; full Fountain overflowing with all graces; glorious Offspring of great God; Thyself great God. Great God, let all things that are in heaven above and in earth beneath bless Thee, for Thou art great and great is Thy Name. O unfading Beauty of the most high God, and purest Brightness of Eternal Light; O Life enlivening all life, O Light enlightening all light, and sustaining in eternal splendour the thousand thousand thousands of lights that blaze before the Throne of Thy Divine Majesty, on from the distant dawn of their first early shining. O Thou welling Fountain, hidden from mortal sight in the eternal and exhaustless outgushing of Thy fresh limpid floods, Whose springs have no beginning, Whose deeps are deep and infinitely deep, Whose height attains no limit, Whose breadth broadens onwards marginless for ever, Whose purity is unruffled through eternity! The Bosom of unfathomable God pours thee forth from the unsearchable abyss of His own profound, Life begetting Life, Light begetting Light, God begetting God, eternal God begetting eternal God, infinite God, God infinite and in all things coequal with Himself. And, Of Thy fulness we have all received (St. John i. 16).

Thee too, all-plentiful Spring of every good, priceless Light of sevenfold grace, Thee, O most merciful Spirit, I implore to vouchsafe to illuminate me by Thy visitation, whereinsoever, by reason of my frailty, I have too feebly grasped the truth of Thy majesty and grandeur, and whatsoever of all that I have understood of Thy Divine precepts I have by carnal wantonness disesteemed; so may I correct what is amiss, and, helped by Thee, whom, voyaging over this life's sea of perils, I have invoked to my assistance, may I be guided without shipwreck to the harbour of eternal peace.

Thee, too, I entreat, all-pitiful Father, that, as Thou didst first make me and then re-make by the Passion of Thy only-begotten Son, so Thou wouldst give me to think and love whatsoever tends to Thy glory. I am frail and unequal to my undertaking, but do Thou grant me by diligent confession to attain the grace of redemption and salvation. And whatever work I undertake henceforth, make it tend altogether, by Thy grace, through Thy grace, and in Thy grace, to Thine only praise. Keep me henceforth from sin, teach me to be more constant and courageous in good works; and so long as I live in this body, let me show myself some way Thy servant. And so grant me, after my soul's exit from the flesh, to obtain pardon of all my sins and reap life ever lasting. Through Him who with Thee liveth and reigneth for ever and ever. Amen.

[4] [The clean linen of the first robe: 'Mundâ sindone primæ stolæ spiritum meum involve.' The following passage from the first homily of St. Anselm serves to elucidate the expression: Spiritus enim meus super mel dulcis, et hereditas mea super mel et favum' (Ecclus. xxiv. 27), For My Spirit is sweet above honey, and My inheritance above honey and the honeycomb.' Let us then advance and press onwards to the Divine Wisdom, treading obstacles and difficulties under foot, for that Spirit of His which He breathes into those who make for Him is sweeter than honey; and the inheritance of eternal bliss which He has prepared for them transcends in sweetness honey and the honeycomb. Honey, he says; indicating the souls of the just, which, detached from their bodies, are already standing in the presence of the glory of their Creator, "and white stoles were given to each one of them" (Apoc. vi. 11): whereas by honeycomb he indicates the elect, who shall be after the resurrection beatified in body as well as in soul in the kingdom of God, when at last "they shall receive double in their land" (Is. lxi. 7). For the honeycomb is honey in wax, and represents the soul in the body; just as honey without wax represents the soul without the body.' The simplex gloria' of the next paragraph has the like allusion. The idea is by no means peculiar to St. Anselm; as, indeed, might be inferred from the text, for he writes as though the mystical meaning of the prima stola were not new to his readers. St. Bernard says: There are three conditions of the holy souls; the first, namely, in a corruptible body; the second, without the body; the third, in their body now at last glorified. . . . They have already received each her one robe, but they will not be clothed with two robes each until we also are clothed. . . . For the first robe is, as I have said, the happiness and rest of their souls; the second, the immortality and glory of their bodies' (Serm. iii. In Festo omnium Sanctorum). So, too, in Serm. de Diversis, xli. 12, For the present one robe has been given to each (Apoc. vi.) . . . pending their coronation with twofold bliss.' Nor was the idea of medieval origin; for St. Gregory the Great speaks as follows on Job xlii. 11: And every man gave him one ewe and one earring of gold.' For as we said long ago, the saints receive one robe apiece before the resurrection, for they only enjoy bliss of soul; but at the end of the world they will receive two robes each, for they will have not only bliss of mind but also a glorified body.' The passage to which he refers is this: Prior to the resurrection they are said to have

received one robe each, for as yet they only enjoy mental bliss; they will have received their twofold investiture when, together with perfect joy of soul, they are also decked with incorruptible flesh.' And, indeed, the following passage from the seventeenth Meditation gives all that is necessary by way of explanation: Expectant fideles donec impleatur numerus fratrum suorum ut in die resurrectionis duplici stolâ, scilicet corporis et animæ perpetuâ felicitate fruantur.']

TENTH MEDITATION

[§ 50.] OF THE PASSION OF CHRIST.

SWEET Jesus! Sweet in the bending of His Head in death; sweet in His outstretched Arms; sweet in His opened Side; sweet in His Feet fastened together with a nail!

He is sweet in the bending of His Head; for, inclining His Head on the Cross, He seems as it were to say to His beloved: O My beloved, how often hast thou longed to enjoy the Kiss of My Mouth, addressing Me through My companions: "Let Him kiss me with the Kiss of His Mouth" (Cant. i. 1); I am ready, I incline My Head to thee, I offer thee My Mouth; kiss Me, and take thy fill; and say not in thy heart, "I seek not that Kiss, for there is no beauty and no comeliness in His Mouth, but I seek that glorious Kiss which the angel-citizens long to enjoy for ever." Err not thus, for unless thou first have the Kiss of this Mouth thou wilt never be able to attain to that other; therefore kiss this Mouth which I now offer thee, for although it be without comeliness and beauty, yet it is not without grace.'

Sweet in the stretching of His Arms. For stretching out His Arms He lets us know that He, ay He, desires our embraces, and seems as it were to say: O come to Me, you that labour and are burdened, and refresh you within My Arms, within My embraces; you see that I am ready to fold you in My Arms; come then, come all of you; let none fear he will be turned back, "for I desire not the death of the wicked, but that he turn from his way, and live" (Ezech. xxxiii. 11), and "My delights are to be with the children of men'" (Prov. viii. 31).

Sweet in the opening of His Side; for indeed that opened Side has revealed to us the treasures of His goodness, His Heart and His Heart's love for us.

Sweet in the fastening together of His Feet with a nail; for by this He speaks thus, as it were, to us: Lo now, if you think I ought to fly from you, and so are slow to come to Me, knowing that I am swift and fleet-footed as a hind; you see that My Feet are so fixed together with a nail that I cannot fly from you at all, because My pity keeps Me fastened tight. Nor can I flee from you as your sins have merited, for My Hands, they too are fixed with nails.'

O good Jesus! O Lord all lowliness! O Lord all pity! O sweet in Mouth, sweet in Heart, sweet in Ear; unsearchably and unutterably pleasant; all merciful and pitiful, almighty and all- wise, all-bountiful yet not prodigal; O altogether sweet and kind. Thou alone art sovereign good, beautiful among the sons of men? (Ps. xliv. 3), fair and lovely, and chosen out of thousands, and altogether to be desired (Cant. v. 10, 16). All beauty befits the Beautiful.

O my Lord, now my whole soul yearns for Thy embraces and Thy kisses; I seek nothing but Thyself, even though no reward were promised me. Let there be no hell, nor yet no paradise, still for Thy sweet goodness' sake, still for Thine own Self's sake, would I desire to cleave to Thee. Be Thou my only ceaseless meditation, Thou my only word, Thou my only work. Amen.

ELEVENTH MEDITATION

OF THE REDEMPTION OF MANKIND.

[§ 51. **Cur Deus Homo.**] Christian soul, soul raised from sad death, soul redeemed from miserable slavery and set free by the Blood of God, raise thy thoughts; bethink thee of thy revival from the dead, and ponder well the history of thy redemption and thy liberation. Consider where is the virtue of thy salvation, and what it is. Employ thyself in musing on it, delight thyself in contemplating it; shake off thy sloth, do violence to thy heart, bend thy whole mind to. it; taste the goodness of thy Redeemer, break forth in fires of love to thy Saviour. Bite the honeycomb of the words that tell of it, suck their savour pleasant above honey, swallow their health-giving sweetness. Think, and so bite them; understand, and so suck them; love and rejoice, and so swallow them. Gladden thyself by biting, exult in sucking, fill thee to the full with joy by swallowing. Where and what is the virtue and the strength of thy salvation? Christ, Christ assuredly has raised thee up again; He, the good Samaritan, has healed thee; He, the good friend, has redeemed thee with His life, and set thee free. Christ, I say, Christ is He. And so the virtue of thy salvation is the virtue of Christ. And where is it; where is this His virtue? Of a truth, horns are in His Hands, there is His strength hid' (Hab. iii. 4). Yes, horns are in His Hands, for those Hands are fastened to the arms of the Cross. But O, what strength is there in such weakness? What grandeur in such humility? What of worshipful in such contempt? But because in weakness, therefore it is a hidden thing; because in humility, it is veiled; because in contempt, it is concealed and covered up. O hidden strength! that Man fixed to a Cross should transfix the eternal death that oppressed the race of man; that Man bound to a tree should unbind the world which had been fast bound by perpetual death! O veiled omnipotence! that Man condemned with thieves should save men condemned with demons. O virtue concealed and covered up! that one Soul given up to torment should extricate innumerable souls from hell; should as man undergo the death of the body and destroy the death of souls.

Why, good Lord; why, merciful Redeemer; why, mighty Saviour; why didst Thou cover such strength with such humility? Was it to deceive the devil, who by deceiving man drove him out of Paradise? But surely the Truth, deceives not any one. He that will not know

- 75 -

and refuses to believe the Truth, deceives himself; he that sees the Truth, and hates or despises it, deceives himself. No; the Truth deceives none.

Was it, then, that the devil might deceive himself? Surely not; for as the Truth deceives none, so He intends not that any should deceive himself; albeit in allowing this He may be said to do it. For Thou didst not assume humanity that being known Thou mightest hide Thyself, but that not being known Thou mightest reveal Thyself. Thou didst by words declare Thyself true God, true Man, and Thou didst show it by Thy works. The fact was by its nature hidden, but it was not studiously hidden away from view; it was not done in such sort that it might be hidden from sight, but that in its own order it might be brought to its consummation; and not that any should be deceived, but that what was fitting might be done. And if indeed it be called a hidden fact, the meaning is, that it is a fact not revealed to all. For, true though it be that the Truth does not manifest Himself to all, yet He denies Himself to none. Therefore, O Lord, Thou didst do what Thou didst, not to deceive, nor that any should deceive himself, but that Thou mightest do what was to be done, and as it was to be done, Thou didst remain true in all things. Whosoever, therefore, has deceived himself in the matter of Thy Truth, let him not complain of Thee, but of his own untruth.

Was there anything in the devil, as regards God, or as regards man, in respect of which it might be the more fittingly due that God should by preference act towards him in behalf of man kind in this manner, rather than with open and displayed strength; so that, inasmuch as he was bent on destroying just man unjustly, he should justly lose the power which he wielded over the unjust? Now, of course, nothing was due to the devil from God but punishment; nor did man owe any debt but his own recovery, thus, that as he, man, easily allowed himself to be conquered, in sinning, by him, the devil, so it was due that he should conquer the devil, and that by a struggle even to the death, in keeping justice unimpaired. But this was man's due, as a debt, to none but God only; for his sin was sin not in respect of the devil, but in respect of God; nor was man accountable to the devil, but man and devil alike were God's. And as to the fact that the devil harassed man, this he did not from zeal for justice, but from love of iniquity; by the permission, not by the command, of God; the justice of God exacting it, not any justice of the devil's. There was nothing, therefore, on the part of the devil to make it due, in respect of him, that God should, having the salvation of man in view, either conceal or set aside His omnipotence.

Was there, then, any inherent necessity compelling the Most High thus to humble Himself, and the Almighty to toil as He did for the attainment of any end of His? Now all necessity and all impossibility is subject to His will; what He wills must of necessity be, what He does not will cannot possibly be. He acted, then, from His sole will; and, since His will is always good, from His sole goodness. For God needed not to save man in this way, but human nature had need that in this way it should satisfy to God. God needed not to endure so great toils and pains, but man had need thus to be reconciled to God; nor did God need to be thus humbled, but man had need thus to be rescued from the pit of hell. The Divine Nature needed not to be humbled, or to labour, nor indeed was it possible that it should; but need was that human nature should undergo all this, in order that it might be restored to that for which it had been created. But neither human nature nor anything that was not God could possibly avail for the attainment of the end. For man is not restored to that for which he was created if he be not advanced to a likeness with the angels, in whom is no sin; which cannot possibly come to pass unless he have received remission of all his sins; and this is not effected without the preliminary of a perfect satisfaction, that satisfaction being of necessity such that the sinner, or some one in the sinner's behalf, offer to God something which is not due by way of debt, and which is of greater value than all that is not God. For if to sin is to dishonour God--and man ought not to commit sin even though the inevitable consequence were that all which is not God should perish--immutable truth and right reason of course require that he who sins should offer to God, by way of restitution for the honour taken from Him, something of greater worth than is that for which he ought not to have dishonoured Him [than all that is outside God]. And, since human nature had not this to give, nor yet could possibly be reconciled without payment of the satisfaction due; lest the justice of God should thus leave sin in God's kingdom sin, a thing so repugnant to the order of that kingdom the goodness of God intervened, and the Son of God assumed it [i.e. human nature] into His own Person, so that, in that Person, Man might be God, and thus possess what should not only transcend every existence which is not God, but also the whole sum of the debt which sinners owe; and, since He owed nothing for Himself, should pay this in behalf of mankind at large, who had not wherewithal to pay what was due from them. For

God-Man's [5] life is of higher price than all that is not God, and transcends in worth all the debt which sinners owe by way of satisfaction. For if the putting Him to death surpasses all other sins, no matter what their heinousness or what their number, which can possibly be imagined outside of and away from the Person of God [i.e. God Himself], it is clear that His life is greater as a good than all sins outside of and away from the Person of God can ever be as evils. This His life God-Man, since death was not a thing He owed by way of debt, inasmuch as He was not a sinner, offered spontaneously, of His own treasure, to the honour of the Father; He offered it in permitting it, for His justice' sake, to be taken away from Him, that thus He might offer an example to all mankind that the justice of God is not to be foregone by them even on account of death, the death which is in their case a debt that they must needs of necessity pay some day; whereas He, who owed no such debt, and might have avoided it without any violation of justice, willingly under went it for justice' sake when inflicted on Himself. Thus, then, Human Nature offered to God in that Man spontaneously and not as of debt that which was its own: so as to redeem itself in others, in whom it had not wherewith to pay what was required by way of debt. In all this the Divine Nature suffered no humiliation, but the Human was exalted; nor was the former in any way detracted from, but the latter was mercifully aided.

Nor did human nature in God-Man suffer aught by any kind of necessity, but only by free election. Nor did it succumb unwillingly to any violence from without, but by spontaneous goodness, endured at once nobly and mercifully, for the honour of God and the benefit of mankind generally, the evils by wicked will inflicted on it; and that by no compulsion of obedience, but by the disposition of an almighty wisdom. For the Father did not impose death upon God-Man by a compulsory imposition, but what He knew would be pleasing to His Father and profitable to mankind, that He voluntarily did. For it was impossible that the Father should force Him to that which could not be required of Him as due to Himself; and on the other hand, it was impossible but that so great an offering, voluntarily offered by the Son with such utter goodness of will, should be pleasing to the Father. Thus, then, He exhibited a free obedience to the Father, inasmuch as He spontaneously willed to do what He knew would be pleasing to the Father. And hence, since this utter goodness of will was the Father's gift to Him, He is not improperly said to have received it as a precept of His Father's. In this way, therefore, it is that He was obedient to the

Father even unto death; and that, as the Father gave Him commandment, so He did; and that He drank the chalice which His Father gave Him. For the obedience of Human Nature is exhibited at once in full perfection and in uttermost freedom, when it voluntarily surrenders its own free will to the will of God, and when, with a freedom all its own, it perfects the good will which was therefore accepted because unexacted.

Thus He, Man, redeems mankind, inasmuch as that which He has of His own will offered to God is reckoned as covering the debt which was owing from them. By which payment man is not only and merely once redeemed from his faults, but how often soever he returns to God with worthy repentance, he is received; a repentance, however, be it well borne in mind, which is not promised unconditionally and absolutely to the sinner. And since this payment was effected on the Cross, our Christ has by the Cross redeemed us. Those, then, who choose to approach with worthy disposition to this grace are saved; whilst those who despise it, since they pay not what is due from them, are justly damned.

[§ 52. Thanksgiving for the liberation of mankind.] Lo, then, Christian soul, here is the strength of thy salvation; here is the cause of thy freedom; here is the price of thy redemption. Thou wast a captive, but thus hast thou been redeemed; thou wast a slave, lo, thus thou art made free. And so, an exile, thou art brought home; lost, thou art reclaimed; and dead, thou art restored to life. This let thy heart taste, O man, this let it suck, this let it swallow, whilst thy mouth receives the Body and Blood of the selfsame thy Redeemer. Make this in this present life thy daily bread, thy nourishment, thy support in pilgrimage; for by means of this, this and nothing else, shalt thou remain in Christ and Christ in thee, and in the life to come thy joy shall be full.

But how, O Lord, shall I rejoice in a freedom of mine which is none other than the purchase of Thy bonds; Thine, who didst endure death that I might live? What sort of gladness in my salvation can mine be, when that salvation is none other than the fruit of Thy griefs? How shall I exult in a life of mine, which is mine only by Thy death? Am I to rejoice in Thy sufferings, and in the cruelty of those who caused them? For, indeed, Thou hadst not borne them, had not they inflicted them, and, hadst Thou not endured them, all these my blessings had not been. And, on the other hand, if I grieve over the

79

sufferings, how shall I rejoice in the blessings for which the sufferings were undergone, and which would not have been had the sufferings not been? Truth is, the wickedness that inflicted them was able to do nothing save as Thou didst willingly allow; nor didst Thou allow save as Thou didst mercifully will. I must needs therefore execrate the cruelty of those who caused Thy pains; I must compassionate and imitate Thy death and Thy toils; I must render Thee the homage of a thankful love for Thy merciful free choice in my behalf; and thus exult in safety and confidence in the benefits bestowed on me.

[**§ 53. Man's past condition and present privilege.**] Therefore, poor mortal, leave their cruelty to the judgment of God, and busy thy thoughts with the debt of gratitude thou owest to thy Saviour. Consider what plight thou wast in, and what has been done for thee; think, too, who it is that has done it, and of what love He is worthy. Review at once thy need and His goodness; and see what thanks on the one hand thou renderest, and on the other how much thou owest to His love. Thou wast in darkness, on slippery ground, and on a slope sheering down to the chaos of hell whence none may return; an enormous weight, like some load of lead hanging from thy neck, dragged thee lower and lower; a burden too heavy to bear pressed upon thee from above; and unseen foes urged thee on, spite of thy struggles to get free. Thus wast thou, and without all help; and thou knewest not thy plight, for thus hast thou been conceived and born. O, what was thy condition then, and whither did they hurry thee! Shudder at the recollection, tremble at the review of it. O good Christ, O Lord Jesus; posited thus, neither seeking Thee, nor thinking of Thee, Thou didst shine upon me like a sun, and didst show me in what predicament I was. Thou didst throw away the leaden weight that dragged me down; Thou didst take off the burden that weighed upon me; Thou didst drive back the pursuing foes, and stand forth against them in my, defence; Thou calledst me by a new name, a name which Thou gavest me after Thine own; and, bowed down as I was, didst raise and set me up so as to behold Thee, saying, Be of good heart; I have redeemed thee, I have given My life for thee. Do but cleave to Me, and thou shalt escape the miseries in which thou wast, and shalt not fall into the deep whither thou wast hurrying; but I will lead thee on, even to My kingdom, and make thee an heir of God, and a joint-heir with Myself.' Thenceforth Thou didst take me into Thy keeping, that nothing should hurt my soul against Thy allowing. And, behold, although as yet I have not clung to Thee as Thou didst counsel, yet Thou hast not let me fall into hell, but art waiting still, that I may cling to Thee, and Thou do for me as Thou hast promised. In truth, O Lord, such was my condition, and thus hast Thou dealt with me. I was in darkness; for I knew nothing, not even myself. I was on slippery ground; for I was weak and frail, and prone to slip into sin. I was on the slopes over the pit of hell; for I had lapsed in my first parents from justice to injustice, a road by which men travel down into hell; and from beatitude to temporal woe, whence men launch into eternal. The weight of original sin drew me from below, and the unsupportable burden of God's judgment oppressed me from above; and my foes the demons, that by fresh actual sins they might make me more worthy of damnation, vehemently assailed me as much as in them it lay to do. Thus destitute, thus helpless, Thou, Jesus, didst shine upon me, and show me in what state I was. For even when as yet I could not know or be aware of it, Thou didst teach it all to others, who were to learn in my behalf, and afterwards me myself, or ever I sought it of Thee. The dragging lead, the pressing load, the urging foes--Thou hast rid me of them all; for Thou hast taken away the sin in which I was conceived and born, both the sin and its condemnation, and hast warded off the spiteful fiends from doing violence to my soul. Thou hast caused me to be called after Thy Name, a Christian; the Name by which I make confession of Thee, and Thou too dost own me among Thy redeemed; Thou hast lifted me up, moreover, and raised me to the knowledge and the love of Thee; Thou hast made me have good hope for the salvation of my soul, my soul for which Thou gavest Thine, and, only that I follow Thee, hast promised me Thy glory. And lo, although not yet I follow Thee as Thou hast counselled nay, rather, have committed many sins which Thou hast forbidden still Thou dost wait, dost wait that I may follow Thee, dost wait to give what Thou hast promised.

[§ 54. The soul's surrender of itself to God.] Consider, O my soul, and thou, my inmost self, reflect, how much my entire being owes to Him. Of a truth, O Lord, because Thou hast made me, I owe my whole self to Thy love; because Thou hast redeemed me, I owe my whole self; because Thou dost promise so much, I owe my whole self; nay, I owe so much more than myself to Thy love as Thou art greater than I, for whom Thou didst give Thyself and dost promise Thyself. Grant, O Lord, I beseech Thee, that I may taste by love what I taste by speculation, perceive by affection what I perceive by the understanding. I owe Thee more than my whole self; but neither have I more, nor even this that I am can I of myself give up whole to Thee. Draw me, or rather this whole self of mine, O Lord, into Thy love. All that I am is

Thine by creation; make it all Thine by love. Behold, O Lord, my heart lies open before Thee; it tries, but of itself it cannot; what self cannot, do Thou. Admit me within the chamber of Thy love. I ask, I seek, I knock. Thou who causest me to ask, cause me to receive. Thou givest the seek, give also the find. Thou teachest how to knock, open to him that knocks. To whom dost Thou ever give, if Thou sayest no to him that asks? "Who finds at all, if he that seeks seeks all in vain? To whom dost Thou open, if Thou shuttest the door to him that knocks? What dost Thou give to him that does not pray, if Thou refusest Thy love to him that does pray? The de siring is from Thee; let me have the obtaining too from Thee. Cling to Him, O my soul; cling, cling with importunity. Good Lord, good Lord, cast it not away; it faints of hunger for Thy love; revive it; let Thy sweet election satiate it, and Thy unfailing fondness nourish it, and Thy divine love fulfil it, and occupy me altogether, and possess and fill me through and through; for Thou art with the Father and the Holy Ghost, God only blessed for ever and ever. Amen.

[5] [The phrase GOD-MAN' is familiar to all, and is used here as a rendering of ILLE HOMO' in preference to any such more literal but less usual forms of expression as The Ideal Man' The Model Man,' or The Man.']

TWELFTH MEDITATION

OF THE HUMANITY OF CHRIST.

[§ 55. The Mystery of the Incarnation.] The subject of our Saviour's most holy birth and in fancy is brimful of joy, of tenderness, of edification: of joy in respect of our own exceeding gladness; of tenderness in regard to His sufferings; and of edification because of the lessons taught us. For what more joyful than to behold as Man Him who, as we know, is man's Creator? What, again, should seem to man more touching than to see, as he does, with unveiled eye, that in the Person of this Meditator of God and men, our Lord Jesus Christ, after a certain wondrous and ineffable manner, eternity begins to be, and majesty is shrouded in humility? He who IS everlasting in the Bosom of the Father is conceived in a Mother's womb. Born from eternity of His Father without mother, He is born in time of His Mother without father. He who clothed the earth with trees and verdure, who decked the sky with its lamps, who peopled the sea with fishes, lies wrapped in rags. He whom the heaven of heavens cannot hold is confined in a narrow manger, is fed with a Mother's milk. The Wisdom, whose wisdom has neither beginning nor end, who is Himself the very Wisdom of God the Father, advances from less to greater. He, whose eternity cannot be contracted even as it cannot be increased, exists by measurement of days and hours; and the primal Author of grace, its Preserver and its Rewarder, grows in grace. He who is the object of the adoration of all created being, and to whom every knee is bowed, is made subject to human parents. Let us add farther, if we may, the following: He is baptised; yes in deed; the Lord by His servant, God by a man, the King by His subject. He whom angels serve is tempted by the devil. Food hungers, the Fountain thirsts, the Way is weary, Greatness is brought low, Might is weakened, Power enfeebled, Glory despised and wronged, Joy mourns, Gladness grieves, Majesty is shrouded in humility, and Life in death.'

[§ 56. Hope inspired by the thought of the Incarnation.] O good Jesus, how sweet Thou art in the heart of one that muses on Thee and that loves Thee! I know not how it is--no, for I can not compass all I say--yet so it is that Thou art far sweeter, in the heart of one who loves Thee, in that Thou art Flesh than in that Thou art the Word; sweeter in Thy lowliness than Thy glory. Yes, indeed, it is far, far sweeter for loving memory to see Thee born in time of Thy Virgin Mother than to behold Thee begotten of Thy Father before the day-star; sweeter to think that Thou hast emptied Thyself, and hast taken the form of a servant, than that in the form of God Thou art equal to God; sweeter to see Thee dying on the tree in the sight of the Jews than to descry Thee lording it in heaven over the angels; sweeter to watch Thee amidst all things humbled and abased than high advanced and exalted over all; to know that as Man Thou hast borne a human lot than that as God Thy dealings have been all Divine; that Thou art the Redeemer of the perishing than that Thou art the Creator of all men out of nothing. O, how sweet it is, good Jesus, to go into the secret chamber of one's heart and there call Thee to mind, for our sake conceived without stain in the Virgin's womb, and born without hurt to her virginity; for our sake wrapped in rags, and laid in a manger, bearing reproaches with patience, and insults silently; to think of Thee washing Thy disciples' feet, and wiping them with a towel; praying on through the long night, sweating Thy sweat of Blood; sold for thirty pieces of silver, betrayed with a kiss, captured with swords and staves, bound, judged, condemned to the scourge, led like an innocent lamb to the slaughter, neither opening Thy mouth when roughly used, nor answering when accused in many things; buffeted, smitten, scourged with whips; discoloured and livid with scars; arrayed in a scarlet cloak; crowned with a crown of thorns; worshipped in derision; beaten about the head with a reed; scorned and mocked in a robe of white, and then condemned to death; to see Thee carrying the cross and fastened to it, praying for Thy murderers; given vinegar to drink and gall to eat, reviled by the thief, pouring forth Thy Blood through the five wounds of Thy Body, bowing Thy Head, giving up the ghost, commending Thy dear Soul into the Hands of Thy Father, and enduring all this for us. All these thoughts breed in us and increase greater and yet greater joy, confidence and consolation, love and desire.

[§ 57. Joy inspired by the thought of the Incarnation.] Who but must rejoice and be beside himself with joy, who but must be beyond all measure happy and full of gladness, on seeing that not only is his Creator made man for his sake, but that, besides this, He has endured such hardnesses and such indignities? What more delicious to ruminate upon? What sweeter for the mind to taste? What more joyful subject of meditation? Who is to rob me of my place in a Kingdom over which He reigns omnipotent who is my Brother and my Flesh? What possible issue can ever make me desolate, since so bright a hope confers on me so certain an assurance? How can any sadness possibly have any sort of place in one in whom a thought like this is incessantly kept alive? Nor is the confidence this thought engenders in me one whit the less that the object of my loving ardours is my own Creator. Assuredly it is in every way a safe, and in no respect a rash, confidence, which is created in the mind by the contemplation of our humanity in the very Person of Christ. Why may I not trust that I shall attain to the inheritance of the elect, when I behold the very Creator of all things dead for the sake of me? For me He poured forth Blood from His Side; why, then, should I not be sure that I have been redeemed, when I know that so high a price has been paid for me? And for me He poured forth water also; why should I not feel confident that I have been cleansed from all my defilements, when it is clear that I have been cleansed by the Water which gushed from the Heart of Christ? The one welled forth from Him, and so did the other; and if the one was shed for my redemption, the other was shed for the washing clean of the redeemed; one for the redemption of the captive, the other for the cleansing of the foul. For me, a slave, was the everlasting Son delivered up, that He might buy me an inheritance by His death; how then shall I not believe myself an heir; ay, indeed, an heir of God, and a joint-heir of Christ? (Rom. viii. 17.) Though I was an enemy, I was reconciled to God by the death of His Son; how, then, justified now by His death, shall I not be saved from wrath through Him? Who shall lay anything to my charge, when His charity covereth the multitude of sins? (1 St. Pet. iv. 8.) His Blood cries from the earth, and speaks better than Abel; and shall not the voice of such and so loud a cry move His Father's Heart?

[§ 58. Love inspired by the thought of the Incarnation.]
Far be it, and again I say, far be it from me that I should lack bowels of compassion as I behold Thee, O good Jesus, dying for me. Thou art crucified before my eyes, and shall no emotion stir my heart? That sword of Thine gleams unsheathed before me, and shall it not pierce my soul? Sweet Jesus, what right have I to compassionate Thee? Yet it is none the less well that I should do so. And why should it not be well, since it is evident, if he discerns and judges aright in whom Thou spakest, that if we suffer with Thee we shall also reign with Thee? (Rom. viii. 17.) And in another place, If we be dead with Him, we shall live also with Him' (2 Tim. ii. 12). But that this compassion of which we speak may live and flourish in our mind, need is that it be inspired by an ardent charity; for whom we embrace with a burning love, those, and those only, we truly compassionate in their woe, and

truly congratulate in their good estate. O Jesus, neither my mind can comprehend, nor my tongue suffice to declare, how worthy Thou art to be loved by me, Thou who hast condescended to love me with such a perfect love. Thou hast loved me, and washed me from my sins in Thine own Blood. For if I love Thee much, Thou certainly hast loved me first, and hast loved me more. For by this,' says the Apostle, hath appeared the charity of God, not as if we have loved God, but because He first loved us' (1 St. John iv. 9, 10). He loved when I loved not; for indeed hadst Thou not loved him that loved not, Thou hadst not made him love. I love Thee, O sweetest Jesus, above all things; but all too little, because far less than Thou deservest, O Thou most dearly loved; and as far less than I ought. And who could? One may indeed love Thee, by Thy gift, as best he can, but never as much as he ought. Who shall repay Thee the worth of Thy innocent Blood, which flowed not in drops but in rivers from five parts of Thy Body? Thou createdst me when I was not; Thou redeemedst me when I was lost. But the sole motive for my being and for my salvation was Thy love. What didst Thou see in me, O Jesus, Sweetness of my life; what didst Thou see in me, that Thou shouldest pay so great a price for me? Nothing, nothing; but so it seemed good in Thy sight. As Creator, Thou bestowedst much on me, but far more as Redeemer. O, how lovely Thou art, Lord Jesus; and O, how sweet! Lovely, but to those who see Thee; sweet, but to those who taste Thee. Thou art not known, unless Thou be seen; nor found sweet, unless Thou be tasted. Make me seek Thee; and seeking find Thee; and finding keep Thee; that Thou mayest be the sole sweetness of my taste, the sole pleasantness, the sole delight. Make me know Thee, fear Thee, love Thee, yearn for Thee. Let me not fall away into love of perishable things. Alas, my Lord, that I cannot taste incessantly how delightful and how sweet Thou art!

[§ 59. Jesus the Salvation of sinners.] I am a sinner, O most merciful Jesus. Have mercy on me, Thou who earnest not to call the just, but sinners. Thou Fountain opened to the house of David, show Thyself, and flow forth, and wash me clean. For Thou art an open fountain to all who thirst after Thee; and of all who truly repent Thou dost wash away the stains, returning good for ill, a gift for their iniquity, merit for their fault, justice for their crime, and grace for their sin. King David had experience of this, who, on repenting, heard from Thy messenger the words, The Lord also hath taken away thy sin; thou shalt not die' (2 Kings xii. 23). For he was washed in Thee with the tears of penance, and cleansed from the stains of a grievous sin; for

Thy purity washed out the foulness of the adulterer's crime, and Thy compassion the murderer's cruelty. In Thee was purged that prince of the Apostles, who wept bitter tears for his cowardly denial of Thee. In Thee, Thou purest and sweetest fountain, the woman who was a sinner was made white as snow, and merited to be blessed with so intimate a nearness to Thyself as to witness the new glories of Thy resurrection, even before Apostles, and to preach the news to them. In Thee too was he made clean, who, hanging near Thee on his cross, whilst he owned that he had received the due re ward of his deeds, and prayed to be remembered by Thee in Thy Kingdom, merited to hear Thee say at once to him, Amen, I say to thee, This day thou shalt be with Me in paradise' (St. Luke xxiii. 43). And day after day, O merciful Jesus, how many are there enlightened and cleansed in Thee; raised from darkness into light, from filthiness to purity! O take me, take me home from my long exile to Thyself.

O good Jesus, Thou living and life-giving sweetness, Thou true unfailing health, if I have sown in the flesh, what shall I reap from the flesh but corruption? And if I have loved the world, what fruit shall I gather from such love? O my Lord God, I was wont to pay a three-fold tribute to the Babylonian king, when employed in his impious service. His service is sin; the threefold tribute is delight, consent, and act; and I paid the tribute in thought, in word, and in deed. See with what fires this boiling cauldron was heated (Jer. i. 14), whose face was from the face of the north; when the suggestion of the enemy made the embers burn, and set ablaze the thoughts of my heart. See, merciful Lord, the threefold cord that bound me tight, in mind, in tongue, in body. From the sole of my foot unto the top of my head there was no soundness in me; therefore heal my soul, for I have sinned against Thee' (Ps. xl. 5). Do Thine own work, O merciful Jesus, and save me. For Thou art called Jesus for this only reason, that Thou shalt save Thy people from their sin (St. Matt. i. 21); who with the Father and the Holy Ghost livest and reignest world without end. Amen.

THIRTEENTH MEDITATION

OF CHRIST.

[§ 60. The Son of God, archetypal Beauty.] My heart's voice is to Thee, my Lord and eternal King, Christ Jesus. The work of Thy hand dares to address Thee with loving boldness, for it yearns after Thy beauty and longs to hear Thy voice. O Thou, my heart's desired One, how long must I bear Thy absence; how long must I sigh after Thee, and my eyes drop tears? O Lord, all love, all loveable, where dwellest Thou? Where is the place of Thy rest, where Thou reposest all joyful among Thy favourite ones, and satisfiest them with the revelations of Thy glory? How happy, how bright, how holy, how ardently to be longed for, is that place of perennial joys! My eye has never reached far enough, nor my heart soared high enough, to know the multitude of the sweetnesses which Thou hast stored up in it for Thy children. And yet I am supported by their fragrance, though I am far away from them. The breath of Thy sweetness comes to me from afar; a sweetness which to me exceeds the odour of balsam, and the breath of frankincense and myrrh, and every kind of sweetest smell. It awakes chaste longings in my heart; and delightful, yet scarce tolerable are its flames. For what have I in heaven?' (Ps. lxxiii. 25.) What is my treasure in that celestial shrine? What is my heritage in the land of the living? Is it not Christ, my Lord, my sole salvation, my total good, my fulness of joy? And how, O Lord, shall I restrain my heart from loving Thee? If I love not Thee, what shall I love? If I transfer my love from Thee, where shall I bestow it worthily? O longed-for Lord, where shall my longings find a rest outside of Thee? If my love stir its wing away from Thee, outside of Thee, it will be soiled; and my longings will be all in vain if they glance aside from Thee. For art not Thou loveable and desirable above all things that can be desired or loved? Whatever worth and beauty all creation has, it has from Thee; and what marvel, since Thou alone excellest all things? Thou hast clothed the sun among the stars with an excellent brightness, and brighter than the sun art Thou. Nay, what is the sun, or what is all created light, in comparison of Thee, but darkness? Thou hast peopled the sky with stars, the empyrean with angels, the air with birds, the waters with fish, the earth with herbs, and plants with flowers. But there is no beauty nor no grace in all of them in comparison of Thee, O Fountain of universal beauty, Lord Jesus. Thou hast stored honey with its sweetness, and sweeter than honey art Thou. Thou hast infused its pleasantness into oil, and pleasanter than oil art Thou. Thou hast shed their odours into all fragrant gums, and sweet and pleasant above all rare spices is Thy fragrance. Thou hast set gold among minerals in rare preeminence for worth and beauty; yet what is all of it compared to my priceless Lord, and His fathom less glory, that the angels long to gaze into? Every precious stone and desirable to look upon is the work of Thy hands,--sardius, topaz, jasper, chrysolite, onyx, beryl, amethyst, sapphire, carbuncle, emerald; and yet what are all of them but toys compared with Thee, all-loveable and all-beauteous King? And Thine own handiwork are those precious and immortal jewels with which Thou, O wise Master-builder, didst in the beginning of the ages beautifully embellish the superethereal palace to the praise and glory of the Father.

[61. The nine Choirs of Angels.] Through Thee, for the fulfilling of the behests of the eternal Father, thousands of thousands glide in swift flight twixt heaven and earth, like industrious bees that flit to and fro between their hive and the flowers; a busy throng, innocent and stainless, neither laggard nor disobedient. Through Thee a hundred times ten thousand stand ministrant in the sanctuary of the temple of highest heaven, staring on the Face of Majesty with a clear unflinching gaze, and sounding forth their harmonious ceaseless hymn to the glory of the triune undivided Godhead. Through Thee the Seraphim burn, the Cherubim shine, the Thrones give judgment.

Thou, O Lord, art a fire that burns and consumes not; and, from their immediate nearness to the fires of Thy Godhead, all the sacred choir of the Seraphim are wrapt in coruscating flame, and pour abroad the overflowing of their blissful ardours on the other armies of Thy battling hosts; and of these we in our turn have tasted of the fulness. Thou, our God, art very Light; and the hills catch Thy glory and shed it on Thy people, when Thou dost largely shower forth Thy hidden treasures of wisdom and knowledge on the eyes of the Cherubim, who fix their nearer gaze on Thee. And from them are lighted in their turn the elect subordinated lamps of Thy marvellous tabernacle, which inextinguishably shine before Thy Face, O Lord.

Thou, King of kings, great awful Judge of judges, dost sit above the lofty Thrones, for they have no higher height than Thine above them, Thrones all life and bliss and uniform profoundest calm; through Thee scanning the ways of truth, and in Thy truth giving forth just judgments.

O Lord, our Lord, the holy sublime Dominions worship Thee, expatiating freely in the mysteries of the Godhead, and, enthroned among the princes of Thy palace, sustain, with no loftiness of haughty pride, the primacy of an exalted rule.

O Lord, my God, through Thee the stately choir of Principalities reign as mighty noble chiefs over the army of the skies in the princedom of a sweet preëminence, unenvying and unenvied in their excellency, and fulfil the mysteries of the Divine will as they read the secret purpose of Thy Heart.

O Lord of the Powers, Thine is their might, as they plunge their flaming brand into the necks of the princes of hell; and fear Thee only, lest these should be able according to their will to do mischief for our hurt.

Thine, O virtue of the Father, are all the blessed wonder-working Virtues, whose ministry makes all the whole universe wonder and adore Thee, and, struck dumb awhile at Thy marvellous works, cry out and say, Whatsoever the Lord pleased He hath done, in heaven, in earth, in the sea, and in all the deeps' (Ps. cxxxv. 6).

Thine, O sweet Jesus, are the magnificent Archangels, in whom the benignity of Thy great condescension chiefly works; for, glorious satraps of Thy palace, Thou disdainest not to dispatch them down to this poor world to support and help our lowliness, creatures of clay that we are, and close allied to dust and ashes. Through them, by Thy command, the chiefest interests of our salvation are administered, and the profoundest secrets of Thy supreme purpose are conveyed to us by them; by them come sicknesses and health to the generations of mankind; by them the kingdoms and the empires of the world subsist. And, chief amongst them do we own Thy Michael, the stalwart standard-bearer and the citizen of heaven, who stands in advance of the army of the living God, and brandishing his champion's blade thunders with terrible voice against the marshalled hosts of the enemy. Who is like God?'

And the blessed Angels, so loveable in their innocence, are they not the choice work of Thy Fingers, O Wisdom of God? For on the day of their creation Thou didst deck them with an in corruptible vestiture for the work of Thy holy service. These are the living stars of the higher heaven, the lilies of the inner paradise, the rose-trees planted by the silent-flowing waters of Siloe, with their roots immovably fixed in Thee. O River of peace, O Breath of the garden of de lights, O only Wisdom ranging round about the circling bourne of heaven; by Thee they shine, and burn, and glow in perfect wisdom, in virginal chastity, and in the ardours of a deathless love. Blooming in endless youth, they find in our weakness the sphere of their faithful service; for they lead us by the hand like tender guides, and direct our steps as we travel through this darksome world, and ward off the assaults of the enemy, and whisper to us the secrets of Thy will, and brace up our failing hearts to good, and carry up the incense of our prayers to the altar of gold, and always supplicate the Face of our merciful Father for us.

Thus, merciful Father, Thou hast indeed some care for us, though for a season we are far away from home. And if the tenth drachma which once slipped from Thy bosom and has now been recovered by Thy toils and sorrows have any worth, it is all Thy gift, good Jesus. If there be aught of sweetest sound in this tenth chord strung of yore for the praise of God, it is the persuasive touch of Thy Sovereign Hand that evokes it, when on the ten-stringed psaltery Thou singest the glory of the Father. Sing as Thou singest, O Lord; play Thy sweet music with the swift and changeful modulations of a manifold thanks giving. Strike those nine tuneful heavenly strings, which never yet sounded harsh or sad. And touch that tenth, of lowest note, whose upper part strained and set in tune to Thee sounds joyfully; whilst its lower part, bound as yet awhile to the earth, knows only how to yield dull sounds of sadness and untunefulness.

[§ 62. The desires of the soul aspiring to God.] When, O First-begotten of God, I muse with intensest thought upon all Thy wonderful works, I tremble with amazement; for Thou dost shine forth all-glorious in every way in all of them. And yet, great though they be, and beautiful and very good, they show as emptiness and nothing compared with Thee. Earth and sky and all their bravery subsist by Thee their Creator and Governor, and utter forth Thy power and fulness, Thy wisdom and beauty, Thy goodness and love; and as light excels darkness, so Thou and Thou alone transcendest all of them. And Thou, my God, awaitest me in heaven, the Treasure and the Reward of Thy servant; Giver at once and Gift, Saviour and Salvation. The expected of my soul, what besides Thee has it desired upon earth?' (Ps. lxxiii. 25.)

Why then should I leave heaven for an atom? What is it in all the earth that I have deemed a greater good than Thee, or -a dearer love than Thee, that I should steal my heart from Thee and desire anything in all the universe outside of Thee? Why in all my life have I ever loved any thing or desired anything but Thee, Jesus my God? Why, Jesus, have I delayed, why have I ever for a moment stopped entertaining Thee in my heart, embracing Thee with my whole soul, and delighting all the inward recesses of my being with Thy sweetness? When I was not with Thee, where was I? When my desires rested not on Thee only, whither, whither did they fly?

God of my life, how vainly have my days been spent, how unprofitably have they slipped by! days which Thou gavest me that I might do Thy will in them, and I have not done it. How long the years, how many the hours that I have squandered, living but bringing forth no fruit in Thy sight! And how then shall I stand? How shall I dare to lift my eyes and look in Thy Face at that great reckoning, if Thou shalt bid me give an account of all my sins or of all my opportunities, and shalt demand the issues of all! O let it not be so, most patient Father; nay, let it not be so, but rather let my wasted opportunities--alas, how many!--be buried in forgetfulness. And if, by Thy help, I have husbanded some few of them--their number is small enough, I know--let these be remembered to eternity; and, Father of all love, let at least this my residue of time be fruitful and hallowed by Thy grace, that it may find a place in the days of eternity and be reckoned in my favour in Thy sight.

Now, then, from this moment do you, all my desires, bestir yourselves and fly to your Lord Jesus: fly away; why linger ye? Speed ye to your goal, seek whom ye seek. You seek Jesus of Nazareth, who was crucified' (St. Mark xvi. 6). He has gone up into heaven; He is not here' (ib.). He is not where He was. He is not where His sacred Head had not where to rest; He is not where He walked in the midst of trouble, despised and put to scorn; He is not where He stood before Pilate to be judged; He is not where He stood derided and mocked in Herod's presence; He is not where He hung between malefactors, spit upon, smitten, wounded, drenched with blood; He is not where He lay, shut in by the stone, and watched by the gentile guards. Where then, O where, is the Lord's Beloved? He rests in confidence, and no plague comes nigh His tabernacle. Above the height of heaven, above all the excellence of the angels, He is ascended and gone up in His own great might, and sits on the Throne of singular glory at the Right-hand of the Father, and reigns with Him, coëternal, consubstantial, clothed with the Divine Light, crowned with glory and honour as befits the Only-begotten, in undisturbed serenity, and joy, and uttermost almightiness; Lord in heaven, and Lord in earth. There all the angels of God adore Him, and the one vast throng of the citizens of the heavenly Sion. In Him, their sole centre, all hearts rejoice together, and the eyes of all the good feast on His Face whom all desire; in Him meet all the desires of all the saints, and the whole heavenly city, every way glorious in His Presence, sing their jubilee, their applause, and their magnificat to Him.

[§ 63. The Saints in heaven.] Rejoice, and praise, O thou habitation of Sion; for great is He that is in the midst of thee, the Holy One of Israel' (Is. xii. 6).

Rejoice, ye glorious Patriarchs in your royal Offspring, for all your expectations are fulfilled in Him and He is highly exalted, and in Him, your Seed, all nations shall be blessed, as the Divine word promised you.

Rejoice, ye Prophets, heralds of truth, in Jesus the great Prophet; for ye now see wonderfully and gloriously fulfilled all that you foretold of Him in the Holy Ghost, and are found faithful by Him in all your words.

And you, illustrious Princes of the sky, you blessed Apostles, rejoice in your Master the Lord Jesus, and again I say, rejoice in a familiar joy along with Christ; for, He whom ye once saw in hunger, and thirst, and weariness, and the like infirmities of the flesh, rejected by all, and reckoned with the wicked; see, how victoriously He conquers, see how royally He reigns, see how all things lie beneath His Feet, see how gloriously He shines in the light of His own dominion and the splendour of His jubilee; and how He has you for partners of His unspeakable glory, who of old continued with Him in His temptations, and were partakers of His griefs. Now you adore those dear Knees of His, which were bent to the earth before you, as you sat at the most holy Supper. Now you adore those sacred Hands, with which the King of kings deigned to wash off the dust from your feet, wiping them with a towel.

Rejoice, ye victorious Martyrs, in Jesus the Prince of your host; for now ye possess Him for whom you gave up your lives to death; you have the reward of your struggle now, you have Jesus Himself the Son of God now.

Rejoice, ye venerable Confessors and Doctors, rejoice in Jesus the Master Teacher of the truth; because whom once you confessed before men by sacred doctrines and holy lives, He now confesses you before His Father and His holy angels.

Rejoice, ye Virgins, denizens of paradise and like the angels; for, He whom you loved and sought and longed for, for love of Him disdaining earthly bridegrooms and all the world's bravery--now you behold Him, the Son of the great King, now you possess Him, now you rest in His chaste caresses, and no treachery of the enemy can ever tear Him from you.

[§ 64. The joys of Mary, Queen of Heaven, and Mother of God.] But, amongst all the dwellers in heaven, be thine, O Mary, the richest and the fullest joy; thine, Virgin among virgins supereminent, Rose of celestial sweetness, bright Star above the brightest of all the primeval lights of Divine illumination. Rejoice with supreme and singular joy above all others; for the very Child whom thou didst bring to a human birth and didst nurse at thy breasts, that Child thou adorest, true and living God, together with angels and all the whole company of the citizens of heaven. Rejoice, O happy Mother, for Whom thou sawest hanging on the wood of the cross, thou now seest reigning in heaven with great glory 3 thou seest all the grandeurs of heaven, of earth, of hell, bowed down before His royal state, and all the might of His enemies crushed in the dust. All joy, all joy of joys is thine, thou plenitude of holiness, thou blessed Jerusalem, our Mother, who art above. Keep joyful holiday, sweet Mother, joyful and unending in the peaceful vision of thy Jesus, the Author of thy immunity from sin.

[§ 65. The loving aspirations of the soul to Jesus.] And thou now, my soul, lift up thyself again with all thy best endeavours, and join the thousands of saints who are rejoicing in Jesus their Lord. Fly thither in the chariot of faith and hope, and by the fire of love take there thy dwelling where Christ is sitting at the right hand of God' (Col. iii. 1). Strain thine eye, and see thou in the light of His countenance. Linger about the marks of His blessed Scars, and kiss them one by one with thankful devotion; Scars whence gushed those rivers of the precious Blood with which the only-begotten Son of God paid for thy salvation, and for thy sanctification to eternal life. O Jesus, he who loves Thee not, let him be anathema; whoso loves Thee not, let him be filled with bitterness. Thy love, O Lord, is chaste and admits of no impurity; the savour of Thy love is pure, and draws aside no soul from rectitude; Thy love is sweet, and no bitterness is in it, for it sweetens the world's bitters, and turns to bitterness its sweets. It is not cramped by adversities, and no oppression overburdens it; it sinks not under want, and is embittered by no grief; it is even and undisturbed in bodily labours, careless of threats, incorruptible in the midst of blandishments; in tortures it remains invincible, and it lives for ever more in death. As the miser gloats over his hoard, and the mother delights in the love of her only child, even so, sweet Jesus, the soul that loves Thee sips joy and gladness from the treasures of Thy dear love. The sweetness of honey, the softness of milk, wine with its freshening taste, and all delight some things--none, none of them so please the palate of those who taste them as Thy love charms the souls of them that love Thee.

O sweet Jesus, living and all-desirable Bread; sweet Fruit of the vine; Oil of mingled rarities; gentle Lamb; strong Lion; lovely Leopard; [6] guileless Dove; swift Eagle; Star of the morning; Sun of eternity; Angel of peace; fontal Light of the sempiternal lights; let my every sense conspire to praise Thee, and love Thee, delight in Thee, and admire Thee; Thee, the God of my heart and my portion, Christ Jesus. Let my heart die to its will, and my flesh to its desires; do Thou live in me, and let the live coal of Thy love glow in the midst of my soul, and break forth into a consuming fire; let Thy grace foster and nourish it in me, that it burn continually on my heart's altar; let it glow in my inmost marrow, and rage in all the recesses of my soul; and in the perfect day let it be found perfected in Thee. In the day when Thou shalt see me stripped of this clothing of mortality, which I now carry about with me, let Thy Love enfold me, and be for a garment of beauty to my soul; that it be found not naked, but clothed upon, and have wherewithal to hide its infirmities from thine Eye. And that strange, that other fire, the fire that shall burn Thine adversaries; let the fervour of Thy love keep it far from me, and raise my soul to Thee, her Creator, and plunge her deep in the ocean of Thy Light Divine. Jesus, my

Lord, let all who love Thee be filled with Thy benedictions; and coming home to Thee let their names be written in heaven, that they may have peace under the covert of Thy wings' (Ps. lxii. 8). To Thee therefore, only-begotten of God, be with the Eternal Father, and the Holy Ghost, unceasing praise, inviolable beauty, and Kingdom never to be moved, enduring for ever and for evermore. Amen.

[6] [Formosa Panthera. The following passage from Hugh of St. Victor, De Bestiis et Aliis Rebus, lib. ii. cap. xxiii., may interest the reader; it is entitled De Pantheræ Natura. There is an animal called panthera, of various colour, but exceeding beautiful and of great gentleness. It is said to be the enemy of none but the dragon. When it has eaten and satisfied itself with all sorts of prey, it betakes itself to its lair, and lays it down and sleeps for three days. And then rising from sleep, it forthwith raises a great cry on high, and sends forth at the same time an odour of exceeding sweetness, so sweet an odour as to surpass all pigments and all aromatic drugs. When, then, they hear its voice, all beasts from far and near gather together and follow its exceeding sweetness. The dragon, however, and only the dragon, on hearing its voice hides terror-stricken in its earthy caves; and there, unable to bear the strength of its odour, coils itself together, and lies dull and stupid, motionless and spiritless, as though it were dead. But all other animals follow the leopard whithersoever it goes.' The passage is too long to quote in full; let it suffice, therefore, to add that Hugh of St. Victor draws instruction (1) from the name of the panthera, quasi omnis fera,' (2) from its variegated skin, (3) from its beauty, (4) from its gentleness, and that he quotes Pliny and St. Isidore; the latter of whom (Etym. lib. xii. cap. viii.) says, Panther dictus, sive quod omnium animalium amicus sit, excepto dracone; sive quia et sui generis societate gaudet, et ad eandem similitudinem quicquid accipit reddit. . . . Bestia minutis orbiculis superpicta, ita ut oculatis ex fulvo circulis nigrâ vel alba distinguatur varietate.' Pliny's testimony is as follows: Ferunt odore earum mire solicitari quadrupedes cunctas, sed capitis torvitate terreri. Quamobrem occultato eo reliqua dulcedine invitatas corripiunt' (H. N. lib. viii. cap. xxiii.). And Ælian gives a like testimony, but at too great length to be quoted in this place. The reference is De Naturâ Animalium, lib. v. cap. xl.]

FOURTEENTH MEDITATION

[§ 66.] Set as we are in the midst of snares, we all too easily grow cold and remiss in our longings after heaven. We have need, therefore, of some constant monitor, whose use shall be that when we have relaxed our efforts and lost ground, we may presently be roused from sloth, and may return to God, our true and highest good. It was not, therefore, from rash presumption, but from a great love for my God that I applied myself to the compilation of this little work; that I might always have about me, collected out of the choicest sayings of the holy fathers, a brief word or two ready to hand about my God; so that whenever I find I am growing cold, I may read, and reading be inflamed to love of Him.

I. Of the wonderful Being of God. Be present with me now, O God; Thou whom I seek, whom I love, whom I confess with heart and mouth, and adore with all my powers. My mind, bound by all vows to Thee, inflamed with love of Thee, breathing after Thee, yearning after Thee, longing to see Thee, Thee only, knows no other sweetness than to speak of Thee, hear of Thee, write of Thee, speculate on Thee, and muse anon on Thy glory in the heart's deepest depth, that the sweet thought of Thee may be some little solace and repose to me in the midst of the whirl and turmoil of this present state. Thee, therefore, I invoke, O most desired Lord; to Thee I cry with a mighty cry in my inmost heart. Yes, indeed; invoking Thee, I invoke Thee in myself; for, but that Thou wert in me, I should not have been, and but that I was in Thee, Thou hadst not been in me. Thou art in me, since Thou dwellest in my memory; by it I know Thee, in it I find Thee, when I call Thee to mind, and when in Thee I delight concerning Thee, through Whom are all things and in Whom are all things.

Thou, O Lord, fillest heaven and earth; sustaining all things, but without effort; filling all things, but without contraction of Thyself; ever active, yet ever at rest; gathering together, yet needing nothing; seeking, though Thou lackest nothing; loving, but without distraction; jealous, yet free from care. Thou repentest, but art never sorry; Thou art angry, yet undisturbed. Thou changest Thy dealings, but alterest not Thy purpose. Thou recoverest what Thou findest, and Thou hast never lost. Never in want, yet Thou rejoicest in gain. Never greedy, yet Thou exactest usury. Thou payest in excess to whom Thou owest not, and ever receivest in excess, but only that Thou mayest owe. And who has anything that is not Thine? Owing nothing, Thou payest debts; paying what is due from Thee, Thou owest nothing. Thou art everywhere, and everywhere art entire. Perceived Thou mayest be, but Thou canst never be seen. In no place art Thou other wise than present, and yet Thou art far from the thoughts of the unjust. Nor art Thou absent in the place whence Thou art far removed; for though Thou be not there to bless, yet Thou art there to punish. Unmoved and unmoving dost Thou stand, and yet we follow after Thee, and following can not overtake Thee. Thou holdest all things, fillest all things, enfoldest all things, surpassest all things, and sustainest all things. Thou teachest the hearts of the faithful without sound of words. Undisturbed by reach of distance, unchanged by lapse of tune, tideless and ebbless, Thou makest the inaccessible light Thy dwelling, which no man hath seen nor can see' (1 Tim. vi. 16). Quiescent and self-sustained, still Thou evermore encirclest all. Thou canst not be parted and divided, for Thou art truly one; nor art Thou here, and there, and there again; but Thou All enfoldest all, fulfillest all, enlightenest and possessest all.

[§ 67.] II. Of the science of God, and the inadequacy of human speech to utter it. Though the whole world were filled with books, the unutterable science of Thy Being cannot have due utterance. For since Thou art all unspeakable, no writer's and no limner's skill could describe Thee or portray Thee. Thou art the Fountain of Light Divine, and the Sun of eternal splendour. Great Thou art without quantity, and therefore infinite; good without quality, and therefore the truly and supremely good; and none is good but Thou and Thou alone. Thy will is act; for power and will are one in Thee. By Thy mere will Thou madest all things out of nothing. Thou dost fulfil all creation without any lack whatever, and dost control it without toil, and rule it without fatigue; and there is nothing that can disturb the order of Thy Kingdom, whether in little things or in great Thou art contained in all places, independently of place; and enfoldest all things without distribution of Thyself; and neither moving nor inert art present everywhere. Thou art not the Author of evil, for Thou canst not make it. There is no thing that Thou canst not do, nor didst Thou ever repent of anything that Thou hadst done. As we were made by Thy goodness, so are we punished by Thy justice, and set free by Thy tender mercy. Thy omnipotence controls all things, and rules and fills what is has created. Nor, though we say that Thou fillest all things, do all things therefore hold Thee, for they are rather held by Thee. Thou dost neither pervade all things, one by one sever ally; nor must we suppose that each separate object holds Thee by way of proportion to its size, the greatest more and the least less, since rather Thou art all Thyself in all things, and all things are in Thee. Thy omnipotence embraces all things; nor can any one find a recess wherein to avoid Thy power. For he who has Thee not at peace with him will never escape Thee in Thine anger.

[§ 68.] III. Of the desire of a soul thirsting after God. Thee, therefore, O God of tenderest mercy, I invoke into my soul, the soul which Thou dost furnish for Thy reception by the very desire Thou breathest into it. Enter into it, I pray Thee, and fit it for Thyself; that what Thou hast made and remade, Thou mayest hold and keep; that so I may keep Thee as a signet upon my heart. I implore Thee, O most merciful, forsake not him that calls upon Thee; because, or ever I called on Thee, Thou didst call me, and didst seek for me, that Thy servant might seek Thee; and seeking might find Thee, and finding might love Thee. I have sought Thee, and I have found Thee, Lord; and now I desire to love Thee. Increase this my desire, and give what I seek; for wert Thou to give me all that Thou didst ever make, that all were not enough without the gift of Thyself. Therefore, O my God, give me Thyself; restore me Thyself. See how I love Thee; and if it is too little, let me love Thee more. I am enthralled by love of Thee; I burn with longings after Thee; I am entranced with the sweet thought of Thee. When my mind sighs .after Thee, and dwells on Thy unspeakable mercy, lo, the very burden of the flesh weighs less, the tumult of distracting thoughts is lulled, mortality with its weary load palsies me not according to its wont; all is hushed, all is still; my heart glows, my soul exults; my memory is quickened,. my understanding filled with light; and my whole spirit, set on fire with desire of the vision of Thee, finds itself ravished with love of the things unseen. O let my soul take wings like an eagle's, let it fly and not faint; let it fly till it reaches the goodliness of Thy dwelling and Thy glorious throne; and there, seated at the table of refreshment set for the citizens above, let it feast on Thine Eyes, and take its full in the place of pasture hard by the rivers of plenty. Be Thou our exultation, for Thou art our hope, our salvation, and our redemption. Be Thou our joy, for Thou wilt be our prize. Ever, ever let my soul seek Thee, and grant Thou that seeking Thee she miss not her goal.

[§ 69.] IV. Of the misery of a soul that loves not and that seeks not our Lord Jesus Christ. Ah, wretched soul that seeks not Christ, nor loves Him; it lies barren and parched and sad. O God, his very life is loss who loves not Thee. He who cares to live, but not for Thee, is nothing and nothing worth. He who refuses to live to Thee is dead. He who is not wise in Thee is all unwise. O most compassionate Jesus, I commend myself to Thee. I yield and resign myself to Thee; for in Thee is my wisdom, my life, my all. I confide in Thee, I trust in Thee, I place all my hope in Thee; for through Thee I shall rise again, and live, and find my rest. I desire Thee, I love Thee and adore Thee; for with Thee shall I dwell, and reign, and be happy for ever. The soul that seeks Thee not, nor loves Thee, loves the world, serves sin, and is slave to vices; is never at rest and never safe. O most Merciful, let my mind be ever busied in Thy service; and all through this my pilgrimage let my heart burn with the fires of Thy love; let my spirit repose in Thee, O my God; let it in all its fancy flights muse upon Thee; let it sing Thy praises with jubilant joy, and so find consolation in its banishment. Let my soul fly and nestle under the shadow of Thy wings, safe from the billows of this life of cares. Let my heart, that sea troubled with great waves, rest itself in Thee and be calm. O Thou, who art rich in all divinest dainties; Thou, God and most bountiful dispenser of heavenly satisfaction, do Thou give refreshment to the weary, call the wanderer to his home, unbind the captive, restore the broken hearted. I pray Thee, by the bowels of that mercy of Thine, whereby as the Orient from on high Thou hast visited us, bid the door open to the poor wretch that knocks, and so let him enter in with unfettered step to Thee, and rest himself in Thee, and regale himself on Thee, the Bread of heaven; for Thou art the Bread and the Fountain of life, Thou art the Light of eternal brightness, Thou art the all and the very source of being of the good who love Thee.

[§ 70.] V. Of the desire of the soul. O God, the Light of all hearts that see Thee, the Life of all souls that love Thee, the Inspiration of all thoughts that seek Thee; grant me this, to cling fast to Thy holy love. Come, I pray Thee, into my heart, and inebriate it with the fulness of Thy pleasures, that so I may forget these things of time. It is shame and grief to me to endure the doings of this naughty world. What I see is sad, and all that I hear of transitory things is grief to me. Help me, O Lord my God, and put joy in my heart; come to me, that I may see Thee. But the dwelling of my soul is all too narrow till Thou come to it, and it be enlarged by Thee. It is all a ruin; build it up again. It contains very much, as I confess and know, which cannot but offend Thine eyes; but who shall cleanse it, or to whom else shall I cry but Thee? Cleanse Thou me from my secret sins, O Lord; and from those of others spare Thy servant' (Ps. xviii. 13). Make me, O sweet Christ, good Jesus, make me, I pray Thee, from love and desire of Thee, to lay aside the burden of carnal desires and earthly concupiscences. Let my soul rule the flesh, my reason the soul, Thy grace my reason; and then subdue me both inwardly and outwardly to Thy will. Grant me that my heart, and my tongue, and all my bones may praise Thee. Enlarge my mind, and raise my heart's vision on high, and so let my soul rise with swift flight of thought to Thee, Thee the eternal Wisdom that presidest over all. Loose me, I beseech Thee, from the cords that bind me, that, rising clear of all things here below, I may hurry home to Thee, cling to Thee alone, and rest in Thee alone.

[71.] VI. Of the happiness of the soul set free from her earthly prison. Happy the soul that, loosed from her earthly prison, seeks heaven with unhampered wing; happy the soul that sees Thee face to face, O dearest Lord; that is touched by no fear of death, but gathers gladness from the incorruptible stores of the glory that cannot fail. Set free from toil and care, she fears no foe now, dreads no death now. She has Thee for her own; Thee, the merciful Lord, whom she long sought and ever loved; and, associated with the hymning choirs, sings through eternity sweet songs of cease less festival to the praise of Thy glory, O Christ, King of glory, O Lord Jesus. For she is inebriated with the plenteousness of Thy house, and Thou givest her to drink of the torrent of Thy pleasures. O happy society of the citizens on high, O happy concourse of all returners to Thee from the weary toil of this our pilgrimage to the loveliness of perfect splendour, to the excellency of perfect grace, where Thy lieges, O Lord, be hold Thee evermore. There nothing that can distract the mind is given the ear to hear. O, what chants are chanted there! What instruments of music there are there! What songs, what melodies without end are sung out there! There sweet-voiced organs sound ever to the hymns, and angels' tenderest melodies, and songs of songs full wonderful, which by the citizens on high are tuned forth to Thy praise and glory. No bitterness, no gall- like harshness, finds place in that Thy realm; for there evil and evil one are not. There is no assailing foe, nor no wantonness of sin there. There is no want there, no uncomeliness, no strife, no insolence, no wrangling, no fear, no uneasiness, no pain, no doubt, no violence, no discord; but peace profound, and perfect love, and jubilation, and eternal praise of God, and unanxious rest for ever, and joy in the Holy Ghost for evermore. O, how blessed shall I be if I hear those Thy people's jocund melodies, and their sweet hymns pouring forth with due honour praises to the most high Trinity! Happy, ay, too happy, shall I be, if I, this very self of mine, shall merit to sing to the Lord Jesus one of the dear songs of Sion.

[§ 72.] VII. Of the joy of Paradise. O life all life; O eternal and eternally-blessed life, where is joy without grief, rest without labour, honour without apprehension, riches without loss, life without death, perpetuity without decay, happiness without disaster; where are all good things in perfect charity; where is beauty and the vision face to face; where is plenitude of science in all and pervading all; where God's goodness is beheld, and the Light enlightening all is glorified by the saints; where the present Majesty of God is discerned, and the eyes of all who gaze upon it are satisfied with that their food of life; where they ever see and long to see, and long without anxious care, and are filled without satiety; where the true Sun of justice replenishes all with the wonderful vision of His beauty, and so enlightens all the denizens of the celestial land that they themselves shine with a light enkindled by God, a light enlightening beyond all the glory of this our sun, and be yond all the splendours of a universe of stars, those who, reposing on the immortal Godhead, are thus made immortal and incorruptible, according to the promise of our Saviour Lord, Father, I will that where I am, they also whom Thou hast given Me may be with Me; that they may see My glory' (St. John xvii. 24); that they all may be one, as Thou, Father, in Me, and I in Thee, that they also may be one in Us' (ib. 21).

[§ 73.] VIII. Of the kingdom of heaven. O kingdom of heaven, O kingdom most blessed, O kingdom that knows not death, O kingdom without end; where are no successions of ages all through eternity; where perpetual nightless day knows no measurement by time; where the conqueror warrior, after finished toil, is laden with unspeakable gifts--

Where crowns undying wreathe the noble brow.'

O that, my load of sins removed, the Divine compassion would bid me, the last and least of Christ's servants, lay down this load of flesh, that so I might pass away into the endless joys of His Kingdom, and rest me there, and join the all-holy choirs, and with blissful spirits pay court to the glory of our Creator, and see the face of God close present, and be touched by no fear of death, and rejoice untroubledly in the incorruption of an en during immortality, and united with

Him who knoweth all things, lose all my blindness and ignorance, and count all that is of earth of little moment, and care not to look back upon or any more remember this valley of tears, with its toilsome life, its life subject to corruption, its life full of all bitterness, its life attended by ills and tyrannised by the powers of hell; this life, with its swelling humours, its parching fevers, its cankering riches, its surfeiting meats, its emaciating hunger, relaxing levity, consuming sorrows, and pinching care; this life, in which security blunts, wealth puffs up, poverty brings low, youth elates, old age bends double, weakness breaks, sorrow crushes, the devil plots, and the world flatters; whilst the flesh is seduced by pleasure, the soul blinded, and the whole man thrown into disorder. When, lo, amidst these so many and so great ills death steals on us, steals on us like a thief, and so effectually puts an end to earthly joys, that when they cease to be, they are reckoned not even to have had a being.

[§ 74.] IX. God comforts the sorrowing soul after her great griefs. But what praises or what return of thanks can we find it in our power to render unto Thee our God, who, in the very midst of the so bitter griefs that harass our mortality, never ceasest to console us with the wonderful visitations of Thy grace? Lo, here I am, a poor wretch full of many sorrows; and while I look forward fearfully to the end of this my life, while I review my sins, while I dread Thy judgment of me, while I think of the hour of death, while I shudder at the torments of hell, while I know not with what sort of strictness and scrutiny Thou art weighing all my works, and am profoundly ignorant of the sort of end that is to close it all; while, in short, I revolve all this and much besides in the depth of my heart; Thou, Thou, O Lord God, art close at hand to console me with Thy wonted mercy, and amidst these my complaints, these my excessive moanings and sighs deep drawn from the bottom of my heart, dost lift up my sad and anxious mind above the tops of the hills unto the garden of spices, and there settest me in a place of pasture beside the rivers of sweet waters, and preparest before me a table of manifold entertainment to refresh my wearied spirit and gladden my sad heart; and thus at last revived with these dainties and raised above the heights of the earth, I rest at last in Thee, in Thee, true Peace.

FIFTEENTH MEDITATION [7]

OF THE MEMORY OF PAST BENEFITS FROM CHRIST, OF THE EXPERIENCE OF PRESENT BENEFITS, AND OF THE HOPE OF FUTURE.

[§ 75. On the subjects of meditation.] No one should be tired of listening to what may rouse us to the love of God. Now we read in the Gospel that there were two sisters who loved their Lord with an ardent devotion; and although each of the two loved both God and her neighbour, yet Martha's special occupation was to attend upon her neighbours, whilst Mary drank from the very Fount itself of love.

Now to the love of God there appertain two things: devotion in heart, and devotion in act. And act consists in the practical exercise of virtues, whilst the heart's devotion revels in the taste of spiritual sweetness. The exercise of virtues has its praise in a fixed rule of life, in fasts, in vigils, in labour, in reading, in prayer, in silence, in poverty, and the rest; whereas affective devotion is nourished by salutary meditation.

And that the dearest love of Jesus may grow by affection in your heart, you have need of a three fold meditation; a meditation, that is to say, on things past, things present, and things to come; a meditation based on our remembrance of the past, our experience of the present, and our contemplation of the future.

[§ 76. The Annunciation.] When, therefore, your mind has been purged from tumultuous thoughts by that practical exercise of virtues, then turn your cleansed eyes back to the past, and first of all enter with blessed Mary into her chamber, and unroll the sacred books in which are foretold a virgin's maternity and the birth of Christ. Then wait, expecting the arrival of the angel, that you may see him enter, and hear him salute her; that then, trans ported with ecstasy and wonder, you may with the greeting angel greet Mary, thy dearest Queen, saying with heart and voice, Hail, Mary, full of grace; the Lord is with thee!' (St. Luke i. 27.) Say it over and over again, and ask yourself what this fulness of grace may be, whence all the whole world has gathered grace; what may be the meaning of the Word was made

Flesh.' O muse, and wonder that the Lord who fills earth and heaven is shut up in that, a maiden's, womb, whom the Father has sanctified, the Son taken for His mother, the Holy Ghost overshadowed. O dearest Queen, with what draughts of sweetness wast thou filled, with what fires of love wast thou inflamed, when in thy soul and in thy flesh thou didst own the Presence of so great a Majesty, He of thy flesh taking Flesh to Himself, and after the model of thy sacred limbs clothing Himself with limbs, wherein dwelt corporally all the fulness of the Godhead. And all this, virgin, in your behalf, that you might love the Virgin whom you have taken as a pattern for imitation, and the Virgin's Son, to whom you are espoused.

[§ 77. The Visitation, Nativity, and Adoration of the Kings.] And now, go up with your dearest Queen into the mountainous country: watch the embrace of the Virgin and of her that was barren, and note the lowly salutation by which the servant recognised his Lord, the herald his Judge, the voice the Word, shut up in the womb of an aged mother, owned, I say, the Lord, the Judge, the Word, owned Him enshrined in the Virgin's womb, owned and greeted Him with an unspeakable joy. O blessed wombs, in one the Saviour of the world is rising to enlighten it; in the other, joy that shall know no end speaks with prophetic voice of clouds of sorrow banished from the sky. Hasten, I pray you, hasten; take your share in joys such as these; throw yourself at the feet of each; embrace your Spouse in the holy shrine of the one, and in the other's womb venerate the Bridegroom's friend.

With all devotion follow our Mother after this to Bethlehem, and attend her as she turns aside into the inn; bow yourself down all reverently while she brings forth her Child; and when the Babe is placed in the manger, break forth in cries of exultation, and sing with Isaias, A Child is born to us: and a Son is given to us' (Is. ix. 7), and embrace that dear crib of His. Let love temper bashfulness, and devotion banish fear, and so press your lips to those holiest Feet, and imprint kisses on His Knees. And then recall in imagination the watches of the shepherds, and marvel at the troops of angels, and mingle your prayers with the heaven-taught melody, singing in your heart and singing with your lips, Glory to God in the highest!' (St. Luke ii. 14.)

Nor must you in your meditation pass over the Magi and their offerings; nor leave Him to fly into Egypt unescorted. Let the eye of your devotion watch the Baby Jesus sweetly sucking the sweet breasts of the glorious Virgin-Mother, and after a child's wont laying His Hand on His Mother's bosom, and looking up and smiling at her. What sweeter sight? what more delightful? See Him Who IS, the Infinite, clinging with tiny arms to a mother's neck; and say, O happy, and more than happy, I, to see Whom kings desired to see, and saw not!' Worthy indeed to be seen is He, for He is beautiful above the sons of men' (Ps. xliv. 3).

[§ 78. The flight into Egypt.] Think, and think again, with what thoughts and what meditations that dearest Mother was entranced, as, all joyous and full of rapture, she held Him, her Lord, at once so great and so little, in her arms; kissed over and over again her little Infant, as He gambolled in her lap; or consoled Him in His tears with what lullaby she could, rocking Him on her knees; or, again, soothed Him with industrious care, as maternal love prompted her, according to His changeful wants. You may think the story to be true which relates that in the course of His journey He was seized by bandits, and res cued by the kindness of a certain youth. This lad, so the legend runs, was the son of the robber chief; who, on obtaining his share of the booty, and gazing on the Face of the little Child in His Mother's lap, descried in His all-lovely Face so bright a majesty as that, not doubting Him to be more than human, he was inflamed with love of Him, and embracing Him exclaimed, O most blessed Babe, should ever time come to Thee for having pity on me, remember me then, and for get not this time.' They say that this lad was in after time the thief, who, hanging crucified at the right hand of his God, rebuked the blasphemy of his fellow with the words, Neither dost thou fear God' (St. Luke xxiii. 40); but turning to the Lord, and discerning in Him the selfsame majesty that once gleamed on the Baby brow, and mindful of the ancient compact, said, Lord, remember me when Thou shalt come into Thy Kingdom' (ib. 42). I think there can be no indiscretion in using this pious legend as an incentive to love, without rashly affirming it to be true.

[§ 79. The early life, baptism, fasting, and ministry of our Lord.] And think you that no access of sweetness will be yours if you contemplate Him a Boy with boys at Nazareth; or watch Him waiting on His Mother, helping His foster-father? And what will you not feel if, on His going up to Jerusalem with His parents when twelve years of age, and staying behind while they returned, not aware that

He was in the city, you go with His Mother on her three days' search for Him? O, in what showers your tears will fall when you hear the Mother chiding the Son in words of, so to say, sweet reproof! Son, why hast Thou done so to us?' (St. Luke ii. 48.)

But if it delight you to follow your Virgin Spouse whithersoever He goeth (Apoc. xiv. 4), pry into His loftier heights and secreter retirements, and at the wave of Jordon hear the Person of the Father in the Voice, see the Person of the Son manifest in the Flesh, and the Holy Ghost under the figure of the Dove.

Passing thence, your dearest Jesus consecrated for you retirement and solitude, and for you sanctified the endurance of fasts, showing you how to fight with your crafty foe. What He did here He did for you, and pay careful heed to His way of doing it. Love Him by whom was done what was done; and what was done, that imitate.

Now, then, let the woman who was taken in adultery be present to your recollection, and recall what Jesus did, what He said, when asked to pass sentence on her. He cast His eyes to the earth, lest haply by looking at the woman He should too much abash her; and when by writing on the earth He had declared her accusers to be earthly and not heavenly, He said, He that is without sin among you, let him first cast a stone at her' (St. John viii. 7). O the wonderful, the unquenchable kindness of Christ! He might justly have condemned her; see how mercifully, and yet how prudently, He set her free! For when by that one sentence He had rebuked them, and banished them the temple, think then what merciful eyes He lifted on her, think with what sweet and gentle voice He pronounced the sentence of His absolution. Imagine His sighs, picture to yourself His tears as He said, Hath no man condemned thee' (ib. viii. 10.) Happy, let me say it, happy was that adulterous woman, absolved of the past, and made secure for the future. For, O good Jesus, when Thou sayest, Neither will I condemn thee' (ib. 10), who--who shall do so? God is He who justifieth. Who is he that shall condemn? (Rom. viii. 33, 34.) Yet, yet again let Thy voice be heard, Go, and now sin no more' (St. John viii. 11).

[§ 80. **Our Lords works of mercy.**] Nor will you pass that house unvisited where they are letting down the paralytic through the tiles before the feet of Jesus; and where power and pity are met together: Son,' He says, thy sins are forgiven thee' (St. Mark ii. 5). O wonderful kindness, O unspeakable mercy! Happy he; he received what he asked not for, remission of sins; a remission unpreceded by confession, unmerited by satisfaction, undemanded by contrition. It was the body's healing, not the soul's, that he craved; and, lo, he gained health of body and of soul! Of a truth, O Lord, in Thy will is life; if Thou decree to save us, no one can stay Thy hand. If Thou decree otherwise, there is none that dare say, Why doest Thou this? Why, Pharisee, dost thou murmur? Is thy eye evil because I am good?' (St. Matt. xx. 15.) Certainly He hath mercy on whom He will' (Rom. ix. 18); let us cry to Him, and pray to Him, that He may be pleased to will. And more than this, let our prayer be enriched, and our devotion deepened, and our love quickened by good works. Let pure hands be lifted up in prayer, hands which blood of impurity has not stained, nor unlawful touch defiled, nor avarice hardened; and with the pure hands let a heart without anger and strife be lifted up, a heart calmed by tranquillity, composed by peace, and washed by purity of conscience. But the paralytic is not said in the account to have satisfied any of these conditions, and yet we do read that he merited remission of all his sins. Such, however, is the virtue of His unspeakable mercy, on which it is the height of folly to presume, even as it is blasphemy to derogate from it. He is able to say efficaciously to whomsoever He will what He said to the paralytic, Thy sins are forgiven thee.' But whoever expects to hear these words spoken to him without labour on his own part, without contrition, without confession, or even without prayer, that man's sins never are remitted.

[§ 81. Bethany and the Coenaculum.] But we must go hence and make our way to Bethany, where the most sacred bonds of friendship are consecrated by our Lord's authority; for Jesus loved Martha, and her sister Mary, and Lazarus' (St. John xi. 5); and no one can doubt that this is told us with a view to the special and sacred law of friendship, a law which bound them close in a common familiar attachment. Witness those sweet tears which lie wept with the weeping sisters, and were interpreted by all the people as the token of His love: Behold how He loved him' (ib. 36).

And, lo, now they make Him a supper. Martha served, but Lazarus was one of them that were at table with him' (St. John xii. 2, 3). Mary therefore took an alabaster box of precious ointment. Rejoice, I pray you, to take part in this feast. And distinguish the parts played by the several per sons. Martha served; Lazarus reclined at table; Mary anoints her Lord. Be this last part yours; break in that supper-room the alabaster of your heart; and whatever you have of devotion, what ever of love, whatever of desire, whatever of affection, pour all of it on the head of your Spouse, adoring God in the Person of Man, and Man in the Personal God. If the traitor chides, if he murmurs, if he is jealous, if he calls your devotion extravagance and waste, heed it not. To what purpose is this waste? For this might have been sold for much,' &c. (St. Matt. xxvi. 8, 9). The Pharisee murmurs, for he is jealous of the penitent. Judas murmurs, for he begrudges the pouring out of the ointment; but the Judge receives not the accusation, and acquits the accused: Why do you trouble this woman? for she hath wrought a good work upon Me' (ib. 10). Let Martha toil, let her serve, let her provide shelter for the wanderer, food for the hungry, drink for the thirsty; I alone am Mary's, and she is Mine. She gives Me all she has; let her expect from Me whatever she desires. What? Do you play Mary's part in forsaking the feet she so delightedly kisses, in turning your eyes from that loveliest of faces that she gazes on, and in shutting your ears to that sweet voice of His with which she is refreshed? Still, let us rise and go hence. Whither, do you say? Why, surely let us go, that you may accompany the Lord of heaven as He advances seated on an ass; and that, marvelling that such great things should be done for you, you may add your praises to the praises of the little children, crying out and saying, Hosanna to the Son of David' (St. Matt. xxi. 9).

And now go up with Him to the large dining-room furnished (St. Mark xiv. 15), and find it your joy to be present at the supper of salvation. Let love conquer bashfulness, and devotion shut out fear, that at least He may give an alms to the beggar from the crumbs that fall from the table; or else stand at a distance, and, like a pauper awaiting a rich man's pleasure, stretch out your hand to receive something. When, however, rising from supper He has girded Himself with a towel and poured water into a basin (St. John xiii. 4, 5), think what majesty it is, what might it is, that is washing the feet of men and wiping them; what condescension it is that touches with so sacred hands the feet of the betrayer. Look, watch, wait, and then offer Him your feet to wash, for whom He washes not shall not have part with Him (St. John xiii. 8).

But why in such haste to go? Stay a moment. Pray do you see who it is that has just reclined himself on His breast and lays his head in His bosom? Happy he, whoever he may be!

O yes! I see now certainly who it is; John is his name. O John, what sweetness, what grace and joy, what light and devotion didst thou draw to thee from that Fountain! In that Fountain, of a truth, are hidden all the treasures of wisdom and knowledge (Col. ii. 3). There is the fountain of mercy, there is the very home of compassion, there is the honeycomb of everlasting sweetness. And why hast thou all this, O John? Art thou sublimer than Peter, or holier than Andrew, or more highly graced than all the rest of the apostles? This is the special privilege of virginity; 'tis because thou art a virgin, elect of the Lord, and of all more loved than all. Now, then, virgin sister, leap for joy, go near, and delay not to claim some little portion of this sweetness; and if you cannot assay a higher part, intrust your heart to John as he fills himself with the wine of joy in contemplation of the Godhead, and then hie thee to thy Lord and draw milk from the fountains of His Humanity; and as He speaks the while, committing His disciples to the Father in that all-holy prayer, Holy Father, keep them in Thy name' (St. John xvii. 11), bow down your head to merit to hear the words, I will that where I am, they also whom Thou hast given Me may be with Me' (ib. 24).

[§ 82. Gethsemane and the high-priest's palace.] It is good for you to be here, but we must go. He will lead the way to Olivet; you must follow. And albeit He takes Peter and the two sons of Zebidee and retires to the recesses of the garden, still do you watch from far, and see how He takes upon Him the necessity of our state; see how He whose are all things begins to grow sorrowful and very sad, saying, My soul is sorrowful even unto death' (St. Matt. xxvi. 38). Why is this, O my God? Thou dost so feel for and with me, in displaying Thyself Man, as that Thou seemest in a certain sort to forget that Thou art God. Fallen prostrate on Thy face Thou prayest, and, lo, Thy Sweat is turned to Blood trickling down upon the ground (St. Luke xxii. 44). Why, my sister, do you delay? Run, run to Him, lap up those dearest drops, and lick the dust of His feet. Do not sleep with Peter, lest you merit to have it said to you as to the rest, What! would you not watch one hour with Me?' (St. Matt. xxvi. 40).

But, lo, the traitor advances with the impious crowd behind him; Judas offers the kiss; they lay hands on Jesus; they hold their Lord fast bound; they manacle those dear hands of His. Who could endure it? Pity, I know, fills all your heart now, and zeal inflames all your inmost parts. Let Him alone, I pray you; let Him suffer; He is suffering for you. Why do you want a sword? why does your anger burn? why are you filled with indignation? For if, like Peter, you cut off an ear of one of them; if you draw the sword and sever a foot from its limb, He will restore everything; nay, should you even kill one of them, without doubt He will raise him to life again.

No; better follow Him to the high-priest's palace, and that loveliest face of His, which they besmear with spittings, wash, O wash it with your tears.

See with what pitiful eyes, with what a merciful and what an efficacious glance He turned and looked on Peter, now for the third time denying Him; and Peter turning back to Him, and returning into himself, wept bitterly. O, good Jesus, would that that dear eye would look on me, that have so often denied Thee by the worst of actions and of desires at the voice of a pert serving-maid, my flesh.

[§ 83. The Prætorium.] And now, for it is morning, He is delivered up to Pilate, before whom He is accused and holds His peace, for He was led as a sheep to the slaughter (Is. liii. 7, Acts viii. 32). Mark Him, how He stands before the governor, with Head bent down, with Eyes turned to the ground, with Face all peace; He speaks little and seldom, He is ready for insults, and goes all eagerly to be scourged. You cannot bear more of this, I know; you cannot bear to see there before your very eyes that dearest Back furrowed by the thongs, that Face bruised with blows, that sensitive Head crowned with thorns; that Eight Hand, which rules heaven and earth, dishonoured with a reed. But see, they are leading Him out; the scourging is over; He wears a crown of thorns, and a purple garment; and Pilate cries, Behold the Man!' (St. John xix. 5.) Man in very truth, who can doubt it? Witness the stripes the rods have made, the livid wounds, the filthy spittings.

Know now, at last, thou Devil, [8] that He is a man. I grant you,' you say, He is a man.' But yet you say, What is He?' Ay, what is He? For amid so many injuries He is not angry, as a man would be; He is not moved, as a man would be; He is not indignant against His torturers, as a man would be. Then surely He is more than man. But if so, who owns more than man? He is owned, I grant, as man in His endurance of the judgments of the wicked of the earth; He will be owned as God when He comes to pass judgment. Too late, O Devil; you have found it out too late. Why have tried to work by Pilate's wife to procure His discharge? You spoke not quick enough. The judge is on the bench; the sentence is pronounced already.

[§ 84. The Crucifixion.] Now He is led forth to death, carrying His Cross. O what a spectacle is this! Do you see it? Lo, the government is upon His shoulders (Is. ix. 6). See, here is His rod of equity, His rod of empire. Wine mingled with gall is given Him to drink. He is stript of His garments, which are divided among the soldiers; but His tunic is not rent, but passes by lot to one of them. His dear Hands and Feet are bored with nails; and He, stretched on the Cross, is hung up between thieves. Of God and men the Mediator, He hangs in the midst between heaven and earth; joining lowest things and highest, earthly things and heavenly; and heaven is bewildered, and earth condoles.

And what of you? No wonder if, while the sun mourns, you mourn also; if, while the earth shakes, you tremble; if, while rocks rend, your heart is torn; if, while the women beside the Cross are all in tears, you cry aloud with them.

And O, amidst it all, think of that sweetest Heart of His, how pitifully still It kept Itself, recking not contumely, heeding no pain, refusing to feel insults and reproaches. Nay, rather, at whose hands He suffers, He compassionates them; by whom He is wounded, He heals them; by whom He is slain, He procures them life. O with what sweetness and self-devotion of heart and soul, with what abundant overflowing charity He cries, Father, forgive them!'

O Lord, look on me; here I am, worshipping Thy Majesty, not slaying Thy Flesh; adoring Thy death, not mocking Thy sufferings; musing on Thy mercy, not contemning Thy weakness. Let, therefore, Thy sweet Humanity interpose in my behalf, and Thy unspeakable compassion commend me to Thy Father; and do Thou say, dear Lord, Father, forgive him.'

But you, virgin, who can presume on a more intimate nearness to the Son of the Virgin than the women that stand far off; come with the Virgin-Mother and the virgin-disciple, come close to the Cross, come close and gaze upon that Face, suffused with pallor. What, my dear sister, will you all-tearless watch your Lady's tears? Do you stand with dry eyes whilst the sword of grief goes through her soul? Will you heave no sigh when you hear Him say to His Mother, Woman, behold thy Son;' and to John, Behold thy Mother.' And just as He gave His disciple a Mother, so did He give Paradise to a robber.

Then one of the soldiers opened His Side with a spear' (St. John xix. 34). O hasten, linger not; eat thy honeycomb with thy honey; drink thy wine with thy milk (Cant. v. 1). The Blood from His Side is made wine for thee, that thou mayest drink thy fill, and the Water turned into milk for thy nourishment; and rivers are made thee in the rock, wounds in His Limbs, and a cavern in the wall of His Body. Hide thee in those gaps, and nestle in them like a dove; and kiss over and over first one and then another; and stained with His Blood thy lips shall be as a scarlet lace, and thy speech shall be sweet' (Cant. iv. 3).

[§ 85. The Entombment and Resurrection.] But wait, wait awhile for the coming of the noble counsellor to draw out the nails, and loosen the Hands and Feet. See how he folds the Corpse in those his happiest arms, and clasps It to his bosom. Then could that holy man exclaim, A bundle of myrrh is my beloved to me' (Cant. i. 12). And as for you; follow you the dearest Treasure of earth and heaven, and support His Feet, or hold up the Hands and the Arms; or at least gather up all carefully the drops of the most precious Blood, as they slowly trickle from him, and lick the dust that His Feet have touched. And notice besides how tenderly and lovingly the blessed Nicodemus lays his fingers on the all-holy Limbs, bathes Them with unguents, and assisted by St. Joseph, lays Him wound round with linen in the sepulchre (St. John xix. 38-40).

And now that this is over, leave not Mary Magdalene, but court her society, help her to prepare the spices, and come with her betimes to the Lord's sepulchre. O, may you merit to see with the eye of the soul, as she did by bodily vision, now an angel sitting on the stone which he had rolled away from the door of the monument; and now again, within the monument, two, one at the head, and one at the feet, preaching the Resurrection and its glories; and yet again Jesus Himself, refreshing the sad and tearful Magdalene with eyes so gentle, and saying with voice so sweet, Mary.' At this word all the cataracts of her soul are broken loose, and tears are distilled from her very marrow, and sighs and sobs from her heart's in most recess. Mary.' O happy thou! What were thy thoughts, thy heart, thy soul, when, in answer to this word, flinging thyself at His Feet, and greeting Him in return, thou saidst Rabboni!' What were the emotions, what the yearnings, what the ardours of thy soul, when thou saidst Rabboni'? Tears prevent more, emotion chokes thy voice, and excess of love absorbs every sense of mind and body. But why, my dear Jesus, dost Thou drive me, loving Thee as I do, from Thy sacred and so longed-for Feet? Touch Me not,' Thou sayest. Why, O Lord, why? Why may I not touch those all-desired Feet of Thine, that were burrowed through with nails and drenched with Blood? Why may I not touch them, and caress them with a thousand kisses? What! is He less my Friend now that He is more glorious? See, I will not let Thee go; I will not leave Thee; I will not spare my tears; my heart shall break with sighs and sobs unless I touch Thee. But He says, Touch Me not.' This blessing shall not be refused thee, though it be delayed; go only, and tell My brethren that I have risen again. She ran quickly, wishing to return quickly; she returns, but not alone; there are other women with her. And Jesus goes to meet them, and with gentlest greeting raises them from their dejection and consoles their sorrow. And see; what was deferred before is granted now. For they came up, and took hold of His Feet, and worshipped Him' (St. Matt. xxviii. 9). Linger here, virgin, as long as you can, and neither let sleep break in upon your joys, nor any exterior distraction interrupt it.

But because in this life of sorrows there is no thing stable, nothing eternal, nor does man ever remain in the same state, need is that our soul, so long as we live in the flesh, be fed with some variety of nourishment. Let us, then, pass from our memories in the past to our experiences in the present, that from these too we may learn how deserving God is of our love.

[7] [The genuineness of this and the two following meditations has been questioned. They certainly do constitute twenty-two chapters out of sixty-eight of a work printed in the appendix to the Benedictine edition of St. Augustine, under the title De Vitâ Eremeticâ. But if internal evidence is to be trusted, they cannot possibly be St. Augustine's. On the other hand, there is no internal evidence whatever, apart from their style, which can justify us in saying that they are not St. Anselm's. It is true that their author wrote them for an only sister, and that that sister was a nun. It is true, also, that St. Anselm [see Epp. iii. 67] towards the end of his life gave us to understand that he was the only brother of his married sister Richera; but it does not follow that she was his only sister; still less does it follow that

he had never had another. On the contrary the probability is, that as she had had several children (iii. 43), only one of whom was at that time left to her, so she had had other brothers and sisters, of whom St. Anselm was the sole survivor. In short, there is no reason whatever for supposing, on the ground of internal evidence, as apart from that of style, that St. Anselm is not the author of these meditations, the fifteenth, sixteenth, and seventeenth. And, as to style and manner, the translator can only say that the more he reads of St. Anselm, the less disposed is he to say that the sixteenth is not his, and the more constrained he is to believe that the seventeenth is his; whilst the fifteenth presents no peculiarities which may not be accounted for by the fact that it was written for the edification of one person, a sister in religion.]

[8] [Zabule. Probably for Diabole; either a corrupted form or a corrupt reading.]

SIXTEENTH MEDITATION

OF PRESENT BENEFITS FROM GOD.

[§ 86. The writer's review of his past life, and exhortation to his sister.] I think it no little blessing that God, turning our parents' ill to good, created us of their flesh, and breathed into us the breath of life, distinguishing us from those who fall prematurely from the womb, or who, choked in their mothers, seem rather to have been conceived for pain than for life. And that He further gave us sound and healthy limbs, so as not to be a grief to ourselves or an object of reproach to others, this assuredly is a great boon. But that He timed our birth as He did, and willed us to be born among people by whose intervention we were brought to His faith and sacraments; how shall we estimate this blessing and the measure of the goodness that prompted it? For what we rejoice to find has been granted to us we see to have been denied to men without number, whose lot as men is identical with ours. They have been left by justice, we have been called by grace.

Let us advance further. Recollecting that we were educated by Christian parents, that fire hurt us not, that water drowned us not, that we were not devoured by a demon, or worried by wild beasts, or killed by a fall, that we were nurtured up to ripe age in His faith and good pleasure, let us own that all was His gift. Thus far our lot was one and the same, children as we were of the same father, the same womb had enclosed us, the same bowels brought us forth.

And now, my sister, see by my case what great things God has done for your soul. He made a difference between you and me, as if between light and darkness; keeping you for Him, and leaving me to myself. O my God, whither did I go? whither did I fly? whither did I banish me? Driven from Thy Face like Cain, I lived on the earth a fugitive and a vagabond, and whoever was to find me was to kill me. For what was a miserable creative to do, abandoned by its Creator? Where was the lost sheep to go, where was it to hide itself, bereaved of its Shepherd? O my sister, 'twas a very evil beast that devoured thy brother. See then in me how great was His goodness in keeping thee unharmed by such a beast. How wretched am I, that lost my innocence! how happy you, whose virginity was protected by the Divine compassion! How often was your purity attempted and assailed, and yet preserved unhurt! whereas I, plunging wilfully into all sorts of shame, heaped up on my soul the fuel of a fire that was to burn me through, the elements of a corruption that was to kill me, the beginnings of the worms that were to gnaw me. Recall if you will all those my foulnesses over which you used to grieve, and for which you often chid me, you, girl and woman, me, boy and man. But the Scripture speaks not amiss which says, No man can correct whom God hath despised' (Eccl. vii. 14). O how dearly should you love the God who, while He cast me off, drew you to Himself; and, equal as were the states of both of us, yet despised me and loved you! Recall, as I said, my vile excesses, when the cloud of lust rose about me, and wanton concupiscence enthralled me, and there was no one to snatch me out and save me (Ps. vii. 3); for the words of the wicked prevailed over me,' who in the pleasant cup of love gave me to drink of the poison of wantonness. Natural sympathy with its charm and desire with its uncleanness combined in one, and at an age weak as yet, dragged me along the rough ways of vice, and then plunged me into a whirlpool of enormities. Thine anger and Thine indignation came upon me, O God, and I knew it not. I became the sport of my impurities, they wrecked and overwhelmed me; and Thou didst keep silence. Ah, my sister, consider carefully into what vilenesses and what foulness I was flung by my own free choice; and know that you too had fallen into such, but that the mercy of Christ preserved you.

I do not mean to say that He conferred no sort of good on me all the time that I say no thing here of the blessings I just now recounted as bestowed on both of us alike He with wonderful patience bore with my iniquities. To whom do I owe it that the earth did not swallow me up, that the bolts of heaven struck me not, nor the rivers drowned me? How could creation have endured so great injury against the Creator, but that He who made it, He who wills not the death of the wicked, but rather that the wicked turn from his way and live (Ezech. xxxiii. 11), restrained it? And, O, His grace to follow the fugitive as He did, and to soothe me in my alarm, and, all-despairing as I was, to restore me to hope, and, familiarised as I was with impurities, to attract and charm me with His sweetnesses, and undo the else indissoluble bonds of an evil habit, and to withdraw me from the world, and kindly receive me for His own! I pass in silence over His many dealings, many, and of great mercy, towards me; lest aught of the glory, which is all rightly His, should seem to be transferred to me. For the goodness of the Giver and the happiness of the recipient are so linked together by mankind, even in the estimates they form, as that not only is the Giver praised who were indeed the only one deserving praise but also the receiver. For who has anything that he has not received? And if he has received it by free gift, why praise him as if he had de served it? Praise, therefore, be to Thee, my God; glory be to Thee, thanksgiving be to Thee; but to me confusion of face (Dan. ix. 8), for that I have done so many ills and received so many goods. How can it be, then,' you will say, that you have received less than I?' O my sister, it is for the same sort of reason as that he is the happier man whose barque is borne back by the breezes safe to port with its cargo of merchandise and its lading of treasure; not he who has been wrecked, and escaped death with loss of everything. You, I mean, have your happiness in the treasure preserved to you by the Divine grace; whilst the chief labour incumbent on me is to repair what is broken, recover what is lost, patch up what is rent. Nay, indeed; I would have you be jealous of me, and think it just cause for shame if, after my so many enormities in my past life, I should ever hereafter prove to be your equal; for albeit the lustre of virginity is oft tarnished by some less and occasional faults, so fine is its nature, hateful evil courses, long persisted in, and sheer force of habit, mar the very features of virtues coming after vices.

Now, therefore, see what are the blessings in respect of which you have the sole experience of the Divine goodness; think with what a winning face Christ came to meet you when you renounced the world, with what dainties He has fed you when you were hungry, how great riches of His Divine compassion He has displayed to you, what affections He has inspired, and with what a cup of love He has inebriated you. For if He has not left without experience of spiritual consolations a runaway slave and rebel recalled by His sole mercy, what sweetness must I not believe Him to have lavished on a virgin? If you were ever tempted, He sustained you; if you began to fail, He set you up. How often, when you were parched for fear, did He not stand by your side, a kind consoler! How often, when you panted for love of Him, did He not pour Himself into your very heart! How often, as you were singing or reading, did He not enlighten with His light the senses of your soul! How often, when you prayed, did He not ravish you with ineffable longings for Himself! How often, your mind being withdrawn from earthly things, did He not transport you into the midst of heavenly delights and the joys of paradise! Think of all these things, and turn them over in your mind, that all your heart's love may be turned over to Him. O, let the world be worthless to you; let all carnal love be as dross; forget that you are in this world; for you have turned your heart's intent and purpose to those who are in heaven and live in God; and where your treasure is, there, my sister, let your heart be also (St. Matt. vi. 21). Do not shut up your heart with the silver coins in your worthless purse; for you can never fly to heaven with a load of money about you. Think day by day that you are going to die, and you will not fidget yourself about to-morrow. Let not the future terrify you with its barren waste, nor a fear of coming hunger deject your spirits; but let all your trust rest in Him who feeds the birds and clothes the lilies. Let Him be your barn, make Him your treasury, make Him your purse, Him your riches, Him your joy; let Him alone be all in all to you. And meanwhile let this suffice for the things of the present.

SEVENTEENTH MEDITATION

OF FUTURE BENEFITS FROM GOD.

[§ 87. **Death and its immediate sequel.**] But, He who bestows on His own such great blessings in the present, what does He reserve for them in the future? As death is the termination of our present state, so is it the beginning of the future. Who is there whose nature does not shrink from it, and whose feelings experience no revulsion at the thought of it? The very beasts shun death, and cling to life, by flight, by concealment in hid den corners, and by a thousand other means.

Pay heed, now, to the answer thy conscience makes; and say, what assurance does thy faith make thee, what promise does thy hope hold out, what does thy love expect and long for? If thy life is a burden to thee, the world a weariness, and the flesh a grief, then surely death is thy desire; death that removes this burdensome yoke, and ends fatigue, and takes away the body with its pain. This one event, I tell thee, transcends all the delights, all the honours, and all the riches of the world; if only, by reason of a cloudless conscience, a faith not to be shaken, and a certain hope, thou art not afraid to die; as he will best experience whose soul after having groaned awhile under the tyranny of this fear of death, has at last escaped into a freer air. For this is a salutary foretaste of thy future bliss; to find, I mean, that as death steals slowly on, thou canst overcome this natural horror by faith, temper it by hope, keep it at arm's length by a conscience reconciled and pure; and if so, then death becomes to thee henceforth the beginning of repose, the goal of labours ended, and the end for ever of all moral ills. For thus it is written, Blessed are the dead, who die in the Lord' (Apoc. xiv. 13). Whence the prophet, distinguishing between the death of the reprobate and the death of the just, says, All the kings of the nations have all of them slept in glory, every one in his own house. But thou art cast out of thy grave, as an unprofitable branch, defiled and wrapped up' (Is. xiv. 18, 19). Yes, all they have slept in glory, whose death has been composed and sanctified by a good conscience; for precious in the sight of the Lord is the death of His saints' (Ps. cxv. 15). Yes, indeed; they have fallen asleep in glory, whose slumber is assisted at by angels, and thronged round about with saints that have sped to give assistance and minister solace to their fellow-citizen; for they do battle for him against his foes, repelling their onslaughts and rebutting their accusations; and so, escorting the holy soul onwards and away to the bosom of Abraham, compose it in a place of rest and peace. Not so the wicked; not so those whom accursed spirits tearing from the body as though they dragged them out of some loathsome sepulchre with instruments forged in hell, hurl down into the pit defil'd' with lust, wrapped up' in the filth of desire, there to be burnt in fires through and through, there to be torn by birds, there to be suffocated with unending stench. Truly, the expectation of the just is joy, but the hope of the wicked shall perish' (Prov. x. 28). But what that rest and that peace shall be, and that joy in the bosom of Abraham which is assured to those there resting; and what is the happiness that they expect; no pen has skill to set it forth, for no man living has experienced what it is. They expect, they wait in happy expectation for the number of their brethren to be filled up, that so, on the day of the resurrection, they may all enjoy together their double robe, [9] that is to say, unending happiness both of body and of soul.

[§ 88. The Day of Judgment: the right hand and the left.]
Now scan the terrors of that day when the virtues of the heavens shall be moved, when the elements shall be dissolved by fiery heat, when hell shall lie disclosed, when all hidden things shall be laid bare. The angry Judge shall descend from above, His fury burning, and His chariots as a tempest (Jer. iv. 13), to award punishment in His wrath, and destruction in flames of fire. O, happy he that is prepared to meet Him! And the wretched souls, what of them? How wretched then all they who now in this life are defiled by luxury, disordered by avarice, puffed up by pride. The angels shall go out, and shall separate the wicked from among the just' (St. Matt. xiii. 49), setting these on His right hand, and those on His left.

Now imagine that you are standing before the judgment-seat of Christ, between this company and that, and not yet assigned to either side. Cast your eyes to the left side of the Judge, and view that unhappy crowd. What shivering horror, what shame, what noisomeness, what fear, what agonies of grief, are there! See how they stand, all misery and woe, their teeth chattering, their bare breasts throbbing, their visage full of horror, their features distorted; crouching for very shame, and full of confusion at their foulness and nakedness. Gladly would they hide themselves, but that is not allowed them: they try to fly, but they are stopped. If they lift up their eyes, their angry Judge is frowning; if they cast them down, the horrible infernal pit flares upon them. There is no explaining away their crimes; to complain to their God of too severe a judgment will be impossible; for, whatever His decision, they know too well--their very consciences tell them so--that it is just. See now, O see, how worthy of all thy love He is, in that by His predestination He has severed thee from this accursed company, by His call has wholly drawn thee away from it, and by His justification has purified thee to Himself.

Predestinated, called, justified; turn now your eyes to His right hand; and bethink you, into whose ranks will He place you, that He may glorify you? O what grace, what dignity, what joy and what security are theirs! Some of them set aloft on seats of judgment, others resplendent with crowns of martyrdom, others all white with virginal flowers, others enriched with largesses of almsgiving, others illustrious with sacred doctrine and erudition; yet all, all, one and all, of them are bound together in one holy society of charity. And the Face of Jesus shines on them; no object of terror, but of love; with no bitterness, but sweetness all; not alarming them, but soothing.

Now take your stand in the middle, as it were, not knowing to which company the Judge's sentence will consign thee. O cruel suspense! Fear and trembling are come upon me, and darkness hath covered me' (Ps. liv. 6). If He join me with those on His left hand, I shall have nothing to complain against His justice; if He enrol me with those on the right, to His grace must I attribute it, not to any merits of mine. In truth, O Lord, my life is in Thy will. Right well, then, may your soul expatiate in His love; for, though He might well have pronounced on you the sentence launched against the wicked, He has chosen rather to unite you with the just, that He may save you.

Imagine, therefore, that you are united with that sacred company, and that you hear the sentence from His Lips, Come, ye blessed of My Father, possess the kingdom prepared for you from the foundation of the world' (St. Matt. xxv. 34). And then, the wretches listening to it, that other word of the Lord, full of anger and fury, Depart from Me, ye cursed, into everlasting fire' (ib. 41). These shall go,' He tells us, into everlasting punishment; but the just into life eternal' (ib. 46). O cruel severance! O miserable lot! For, the wicked having been carried away lest they should see the glory of God, the just shall be taken, each one in his order, and set in his own place, according to his grade and merit, among the ranks of the angels; and then shall the glorious procession start upon its way, Christ our Head leading, and all His members following; and the kingdom shall be given up to God the Father, that He may reign in them and they in Him, sharing that kingdom which was prepared for them even from the very foundation of the world; a kingdom whose glorious state cannot even be conceived by us, much less described in writing or by words. This alone I know, that whatever you may wish to have shall not be wanting.

[§ 89. The joys of Heaven, and the joy of joys.] For there is no mourning there, no weeping, no sorrow, and no fear. There is no sadness there, no difference, no envy, no distress, no temptation, no changefulness and no unhealthiness of clime; no suspicion, no pretence, no flattery, no detraction, no sickness, no age, no death, no poverty, no night, no gloom; no need of eating, of drinking, or of sleeping; and no fatigue. What good, then, is there there? For, surely, where there is neither mourning, nor weeping, nor sorrow, nor sadness, what can there be but perfect joy? Where there is neither trial, nor distress, nor change of seasons, nor unhealthiness of clime; no summer too fierce, no winter too severe; what, what can there be but a certain perfect temperature of the elements, and true and uttermost tranquillity both of body and of mind? Where there is no cause for fear, what can there be but uttermost security? When neither envy nor estrangement, what but real and perfect love? Where no unsightliness, what but real and consummate beauty? Where no poverty, what but perfect fulness? Where neither labour nor exhaustion, what but uttermost repose and fullest strength? Where there is nothing to oppress or burden, what can there be but plenitude of happiness? And where old age and disease are never expected, never feared, what but truest health? Where no night is, and no darkness, what but perfect light? Where death and mortality are altogether swallowed up, what is there but eternal life?

And what more can we require? Yes, indeed; we may ask for more, for something that transcends all this; I mean, the vision, the knowledge, and the love of the Creator. He shall be seen in Himself, and seen in all His creatures; ruling all things, but without solicitude; sustaining all things, but without exertion; communicating Himself in some strange way to each, according to his capacity, but without diminution of Himself, and without division of Himself. That Face shall be seen inviting all love and every longing, the Face that angels long to gaze into; and the meaning, the light, the sweetness of that Face, who, who shall tell them? The Father shall be seen in the Son, and the Son

123

in the Father, and in each of Them the Holy Ghost. For He shall be seen as He is, the promise fulfilled in which He says, He that loveth Me shall be loved by My Father; and I will love him, and will manifest Myself to him' (St. John xiv. 21).

And from this vision proceeds the knowledge of God, of which He Himself says, This is life everlasting, that they may know Thee, the only true God' (ib. xvii. 3).

And from these two, the vision and the knowledge of God, there springs a love so great, an affection so ardent, a charity so sweet, a fruition so abundant, a longing so vehement, that neither satisfaction can pall desire, nor desire weary satisfaction. And what is this? What is it all? Ay, the eye hath not seen, nor ear heard, neither hath it entered into the heart of man, what things God hath prepared for them that love Him' (1 Cor. ii. 9).

Thus, my sister, from the recollection of past benefits from Christ, from experience of present, and from expectation of future, I have tried to sow in you some few seeds for meditations, whence may spring fruits of Divine love; only let meditation rouse your love, and let love awake desire, and let desire elicit tears; that so tears be your bread day and night (Ps. xli. 4), until you appear in His sight, and be embraced in His arms, and say as it is written in the Canticles, My Beloved to me, and I to Him, He shall linger between my breasts' (Cant. i. 12). Which may He vouchsafe to grant you, Who liveth and reigneth God for ever and ever. Amen.

[9] [Duplici stolâ: for the further explanation of this, see p. 128, n.]

EIGHTEENTH MEDITATION [10]

THANKSGIVING FOR THE BENEFITS OF THE DIVINE MERCY, AND PRAYER FOR THEDIVINE ASSISTANCE.

[§ 90. Thanksgiving for past blessings, and prayer for future.]

> My Hope, my Light, sweet Lover of mankind;
> True God and Christ, the Life, the Health, the Peace,
> The Crown of all Thine own; fain would I tell
> What for their saving Thou didst undergo,
> Flesh of our flesh, bonds, cross, wounds, death, and grave;
> Whence issuing in three days victoriously,
> Death trodden under foot, Thou didst appear
> To Thy disciples, strengthening their frail hearts;
> Then, forty days elapsed, didst mount high heaven,
> Where now Thou liv'st and reign'st for evermore.' [11]

Thou art my living God, my holy Christ, my merciful Lord, my great King, my good Shepherd, my Teacher of truth, my seasonable help, my Be loved beautiful beyond all men, my living Bread, my Priest for ever, my Guide and Leader to my fatherland, my true light, my heavenly sweetness, my straight way, my wisdom full of illumination, my stainless simplicity, my peace-making reconciliation, my safe protection, my good portion, my everlasting salvation, my great compassion, my all-enduring patience, my immaculate Victim, my holy redemption, my unfailing hope, my perfect charity, my holy resurrection, my eternal life, my exultation, and my most blessed life, Who shalt endure for evermore. Thee I beseech, implore, and beg, that Thou wouldest complete the work Thy mercy has begun in me; for I, the least of Thy servants, not unmindful of the benefits Thy tender mercy has bestowed on me, give thanks to Thee for that, notwithstanding my unworthiness, Thou of Thy sole compassion didst cause me to be born of Christian parents, and didst loose me from my original bonds by the waters of holy baptism and the Holy Spirit's renovation, and didst enrol me in the company of the sons of Thy adoption; for Thou didst give me the gift of the right faith, and hast evermore vouchsafed to increase and confirm it in my heart by the illumination of Thy grace, and by the teachings of holy mother Church; and, O Lord, I beseech and suppliantly pray Thee, evermore increase this faith in me, this true and holy faith, this Catholic and orthodox faith, this most wise, far-seeing and inconquerable faith, this faith so richly adorned with all blessings and with every virtue, that so it may by love work in me what is pleasing to Thee, and may refuse to give way amidst words of strife in time of persecution, or in the day of necessity and death. O God, Thou Fount and Origin, Bestower and Preserver of all virtues, increase in me, I beseech Thee, true faith, unfailing hope, and perfect charity; profound humility, invincible patience, and perpetual chastity of body and of mind. Give me prudence, justice, fortitude, and temperance; discretion in all things, and a watchful sensibility, that I may wisely make discernment between good and evil, between the right hand and the left. Therefore make me rich in holy virtues, so as by them to serve Thee, and by means of them to please Thee in truth; for by Thy grace I am enamoured of their beauty. Give me them for the honour and glory of Thy name; make them comrades of my faith, that they may be its inseparable companions all through the period of my life. And thus make me, I pray Thee, by Thy grace always stedfast in faith, and ready to do all good works, that Thy faith, which my tongue professes and my writings witness to, may be publicly and openly set forth by the good behaviour of an irreprovable life.

I give Thee thanks, O Lord, that though I was an empty vessel, worthless and senseless, yet Thou didst endue me with knowledge and under standing, and didst give me ever and anon some little skill wherewith to edify. Give me, besides, the gift of wise and very gentle speech, innocent of all bombast or pretence, and incapable of elation, by reason of gifts which are all Thine own, above my brethren. Put, I pray Thee, a word of com fort, of edification, of exhortation, into my mouth by Thy Holy Spirit, that so I may encourage the good to better things, and recall to the path of rectitude, both by word and by example, those who walk amiss. Let the words Thou givest to Thy servant be like sharpest darts and burning arrows, to penetrate and inflame the hearts of those who listen to the fear and the love of Thee, Thou Pastor and Ruler of all, Thou Christ and God, who hast called my littleness to this pastoral office for no merits of mine, but by the sole condescension of Thy mercy; do Thou, for Thine own sake and Thy mercy's sake, fit me for this ministry, that I may rule Thy house wisely, and be strengthened in all things to feed Thy flock according to Thy will. Grant, for Thy mercy and goodness' sake, that I may be made a burning and shining light in Thy house; and vouchsafe for the honour and glory of Thy Name that I may merit to attain Thy glory, bringing much good fruit with me from this community of brethren, for to Thee nothing is difficult, nothing is impossible. With Thee to will is to do; Thy will is act. And so with the heart I believe, and with the mouth I make confession (Rom. x. 10), that Thou art both able and willing to perfect to great issues by me, who am so little and so worthless, this work of Thine; I know and am assured that Thou art able to bring forth good fruit and abundant from Thy flock by means of me, me that am so little and so weak. I am indeed a little, frail, and worthless son of man, having in me nothing that can be of service, nothing that can be suitable to so high an office; and therefore, despairing altogether on account of my own littleness and incapacity, I only find relief and breathe again in Thy mercy, in that and nothing else.

But great though Thou be in great things, yet dost Thou show more glorious still in least; and sweeter than ever, more abundant than ever, will be Thy praise in the mouth of men, when, by means of me, who am so little, Thou shalt have deigned to do great things by Thy flock. Send therefore to my help Thy holy angel out of heaven, that he, helping me in all things, may make this work of Thine prosper in my hand; so that Thy Name be glorified in me, a miserable sinner. Rich in mercy, bountiful in gifts, who givest all to all and losest nothing, grant me heavenly and earthly aid in full sufficiency, that I may have wherewith to feed and to sustain Thy flock both in body and in soul, and to welcome without any hesitation those who come in Thy Name, and also to order and prepare for the repose and well-being of my brethren all the places intrusted to my management, as is fit ting and as duty bids. All this I ask of Thee, O Lord our God; for all our blessings are gifts from Thee, nor can we else serve and please Thee save only by Thy gift.

But if haply it is not in the counsel of Thy eternal will to gain much fruit from Thy sheep by my means, then, I implore and suppliantly pray Thee, release me from the bonds of so weighty an office in ways pleasing to Thyself by the disposition that seems good to Thee. For Thou knowest all things, and canst do all things. What do I here? Why do I dwell in these turmoils, if I am not to do by Thy grace some good for the salvation of my brethren? Two things do I seek from Thee, and for Thy clemency deny me not one of the two. I pray Thee by all Thy loving-kindness give me Thy heavenly consolation in my many troubles. For, as to that exceeding heavy burden which has been laid on my shoulders, I have not strength to carry it; I am afraid to set it down. I am straitened either way, and which to choose I know not. O God, the helper of all that trust in Thee, let not Thy mercy leave me nor Thy grace forsake me. O God, keep me; for I trust in Thee, and I confide only in Thy mercy; , since without Thee I cannot please Thee. Did ever any one hope in Thee, and was confounded? (Ecclus. ii. 11.) From the beginning of the world it hath not been heard (St. John ix. 32). Thou art the all-good God, of infinite mercy and boundless goodness, and wert never wont to forsake them that hope in Thee. O show Thy mercy upon me, I beseech Thee; for I have fled to Thee; that they who hate me may see and be confounded, because Thou, O Lord, hast helped me, and hast comforted me' (Ps. lxxxv. 17).

[§ 91. Thanksgiving for past blessings, and prayer for future.] I give Thee thanks, O Lord, that Thou hast separated me from the vain society of this world, and led me on to this Thy sacred office, for no merits of mine, but by the sole condescension of Thy mercy. I bless Thee, O Lord our God, who givest me, undeserving as I am, to enjoy the society and the love of Thy servants. Give me quiet, give me health of body and health of soul; and withal suitable leisure to devote to Thee. Deliver me from the vain entanglements of this world; so that my soul may profit, for the honour and glory of Thy Name. And since it is written, No man, being a soldier to God, entangleth himself with worldly business' (2 Tim. ii. 4); and since Thou dost for this end withdraw from all cares and turmoil the souls of them that serve Thee, that they may be intent on Thee, their only Lord, by night and by day; give those who renounce the world a fruitful and spiritual disengagement, that with the palate of their inmost heart they may taste and see that the Lord is sweet' (1 St. Pet. ii. 3); that Thou, O Lord, art sweet and pleasant, as Thy scripture doth instruct us, saying, Be still, and see that I am God' (Ps. xlv. 11); and in another place, The wisdom of a scribe cometh by his time of leisure; and he that is less in action shall receive wisdom' (Ecclus. xxxviii. 25). But let the all-holy word which issued from Thy mouth inform us yet more fully, You cannot serve God and mammon' (St. Matt. vi. 24); and again, No man putting his hand to the plough, and looking back, is fit for the Kingdom of God' (St. Luke ix. 62); and Thou dost vouchsafe in another place to recall us by an evident instance, Be you mindful of Lot's wife' (St. Luke xvii. 32).

I give Thee thanks, most merciful Lord, that, miserable and most heedless sinner though I be, and have been from the first, and though, beginning from my cradle, I have run through well nigh every course of vice and sin, yet still Thou dost so kindly and forbearingly await me and invite me to repentance; not willing to destroy me with my sins, my faults, my failings, and my neglects. For if Thou hadst willed to deal with me according to my sins, long, long ago had the earth swallowed me up alive. But, I pray Thee, Lord of pity, let not Thy waiting for me be in vain; let it not have been unfruitful all. Thou, who desirest not the death of the wicked (Ezech. xxxiii. 11), give for my past ills forgiveness, and amendment for the present; and, as to those yet to be, ever, ever grant me watchfulness and caution. Give me opportunity and space for fruit worthy of penance (St. Luke iii. 8); open the eyes of my heart by Thy Holy Spirit, that I may see and be-wail all my sins. Behold, Lord, now is the acceptable time, now is the day of salvation' (2 Cor. ii. 6). Have mercy on me, O Lord, and destroy me not with my sins; nor reserve my ills for punishment in that life to come, in those torments of hell, in that fearful scrutiny of Thine. For Thy tender mercy's sake loose the bonds of all my sins before I pass away from this life. Give me a contrite and humble heart; give me the gift of tears. Give me light in my heart, strength in my body, that I may see what is to be done, and, what I see, may have strength and vigour to accomplish all the days of my life. Have mercy on me, O God, have mercy on me' (Ps. lvi. 2). Let not this sinful soul, for which Thou didst deign to be born of the Virgin and to die on the Cross--bid it not, I pray Thee, be separated from this mortal body before Thou make me fully and perfectly repent, and bemoan all sins soever that I have committed since baptism, sins from my very cradle, whether committed knowingly or unknowingly, whether committed from self-sufficiency or from carelessness. So may I in the day of my departure, all my faults cleansed away, and my whole behaviour chastened and corrected to what is good, gaze all secure and happy on Thy all-sweet, all-lovely Face, full of joy and exultation for Thy boundless mercy and goodness.

Again I give Thee thanks, and yet again, O merciful almighty Christ, that Thou hast hitherto been pleased to deliver me, worthless and insignificant as I am, for Thine own sake and Thy Holy Name's sake, from many straits, many tribulations, calamities, and sicknesses; to save me from many pits, snares, scandals, and sins; from many treacheries of foes visible and invisible; from many evils and most serious perils; marvellously and mercifully guiding my life's course between adversity on the one hand, and prosperity on the other, so that neither should the one deject me nor the other too much elate.

For Thou hast put a bridle on my jaws, and hast not left me altogether at the disposal of my own will, having care for me in Thy fatherly compassion, and not suffering me to be tempted beyond my power of endurance (1 Cor. x. 13). Where there was opportunity for sinning, often there was not the will; or where there was the will, opportunity was wanting.

Therefore be praise and benediction and thanks giving rendered unto Thee, O Lord my God, for all Thy gifts and largesses, and for all the benefits which Thou dost lavish on me both in soul and body, and hast lavished incessantly even from my cradle, such has been Thy mercy and Thy goodness, no merits of mine requiring; nay, rather, my sins notwithstanding. But I pray Thee, Lord, I pray Thee, let me not be unthankful for such great benefits, nor unworthy of so many mercies. Be it neither mine, nor the devil's, nor the world's, nor anything's, nor any man's whatsoever, to over throw Thy gifts in me; for whatever would oppose Thee is soon dashed to pieces. Put Thy bridle, I beseech, tighter and tighter to my jaws, and lead me after Thee like some tractable and gentle brute; in nothing rebellious to Thy bidding, but with even and measured step carrying Thee, my Lord, and in all things submissive to Thy will. Bestir my sluggishness, O Lord, with whips and goads of Thine, and make me with my whole heart and energies seek Thy Face all the days of my life. Draw me to Thee, O God, Thou virtue of our salvation, with the rein of Thy mighty grace, and let me not wander loose from wilfulness of mine in places of my own choosing. Let not Thy Image be defaced and blurred in me; for so long as it is protected by Thy care it remains ever noble, princely, and distinct. Have mercy on me, O Lord, on me Thy most miserable and unworthy servant; for I am not like those numberlessly many vassals of Thine, who have served Thee from their cradle; nor like those who, after notorious sins committed, have merited by penance to become devout; nor like the Christian married women, not a few, who do Thee service by works of mercy with utmost devotion; nor again am I like many of those who, in the eyes of men, seem wicked and renegade, but show far otherwise in Thy sight; for Thou only knowest the hearts of the children of men' (2 Par. vi. 30). But if, by Thy bountiful grace, I ever do or ever shall do any good, I know not for what issue it is done, nor with what strict scrutiny it will be judged by Thee. Wherefore, O God, who art terrible in Thy counsels over the sons of men (Ps. lxv. 5), I suppliantly and with exceeding dread implore Thy holy and infinite condescension, forasmuch as Thou wilt have none perish but that all should be saved, not to leave me to the disposal of my own designs, not to the sentence of my own will, nor within the power or temptation of the demons, nor to the erring judgment or the harmful designs of men; but for Thy goodness and Thy mercy's sake, according to that all-bountiful providence which can never be mistaken in its designs, do Thou here and ever, now and always, dispose the days of my life in the order of Thy good pleasure, and by Thy Holy Spirit direct my heart, my tongue, and my actions by Thy mercy in accordance to Thy will; that Thou being my Ruler, and Thou my Guide, I may ever truly study by Thy grace to speak and to do what is pleasing to Thee; so may they conduct me at last to eternal life, through Thy mercy and Thy gift, who art the bestower of all good things, and who art with the Father and the Holy Ghost God blessed for ever and ever. Amen,

[10] [Probably written at Bec.]

[11] [2 The original consists of eight hexameter verses: Spes mea, Christe Deus, hominum Tu dulcis amator, Lux mea,' &c.]

NINETEENTH MEDITATION

OF THE SWEETNESS OF THE DIVINE MAJESTY, AND OF MANY OTHER THINGS.

[§ 92.] I. Wonder at the unspeakable goodness of God the Creator, and the deep misery of man the creature. When I consider what God is, how sweet His Being, how loveable, and how good; when I think how It baffles all resources of speech and all capacity of wonder, and what demands It makes on the reverence and the admiration of every creature; and when, on the other hand, I see and understand what man is, whom very God made to His own Image and Likeness, and whom, furthermore, He created such that as he should always display in himself the image of his Creator, so he might always keep in mind the will and the love of Him who made him such as he is; when I review all this, I am overcome with wonder and with astonishment at the inestimable goodness of the Creator God, and the great misery of the creature man.

I wonder at the unspeakable goodness of God, that being, as He is, most omnipotent and most just, He should allow man to live even for a single hour; man whom He was pleased to create crowned with honour, in order that, as he, man, was more noble in himself than other creatures, so he should ever live, according to the will of his Creator, a more noble life than other creatures. And yet, most wretched and most miserable being, he does the very contrary; inasmuch as, whilst all other creatures ever correspond with the will of their Creator, he always, or at best only not always, contradicts and resists His will.

And I wonder also at man's unbounded misery; I wonder to see that he has so far lost sense, and to such a degree lives like the very beast which has no sense, as at times to lose sight of his Creator, whereas he cannot ever lose sight of himself. I suppose that, unless he be mad, he is never oblivious of himself; never, I mean, so far oblivious as not to be well aware that he exists, and that he is a living and an intelligent being. Surely, it is fit matter for wonder and for unbounded astonishment, that man, so well aware that he possesses all these endowments, should ever lose sight of Him whose good pleasure it has been to bestow all these endowments on him.

[§ 93.] II. The degree to which man may be loved by man, and the reason why God should be more loved than any human being. The man who in this life receives some benefit or other from a fellow man will not unfrequently love his benefactor with so fervent an attachment, and devote himself to his service with such utter self-abandonment, as even not to shrink from facing death, and that more than once, in his behalf, should that benefactor's interest require it. And yet no one is so devoid of sense as not to be sufficiently well aware that nothing which a man may possess in this life, nothing which one man may give to an other, can possibly be retained for ever, but that the owner must forego it before it comes to an end in the ordinary course of things, or, if not before, at any rate when it does come to an end.

But what God in this life gives to man is either such that he can never part with it and that none can ever take it from him, or else it is such that, even though man should forego it, it had been possible for him, by means of it, to merit an existence to all eternity with his Creator in a life of bliss. In this life, however, God frequently enough gives man the means of living according to reason, of loving his Creator as He commands and as is just, of paying persistent and unvarying obedience to His commandments; and no man can deprive him of this good, unless he of his own sole will forego it. Money, perishable money, he must forego, will he, nill he; but, so long as he has it, if he dispenses it as his God has bidden, he will merit by doing so to attain to eternal life.

O the infinite goodness and the inestimable condescension of our Creator! Having no need of man in any respect or at any time, yet of His sole goodness He created man, and creating him, endowed him with capacity of reason, that so he might be able to share His happiness and His eternity, and thus possess with Him joy and gladness everlastingly. And even now, although in many respects man stands opposed to Him, and does many things, knowingly and willingly, which must displease Him; yet does God admonish him to return and sue for pity of his Creator, and never presume to despair, whatever be the sin that he has committed. For He is the Fountain of mercy and compassion; and He longs to cleanse all men, with however deep a stain of sin they be defiled, and having cleansed them, to award them the joy of everlasting life.

[§ 94.] III. God made all things good, but He alone is Good essentially. O dearest and most sweet Lord Jesus Christ, Who art the merciful Lover of man kind and most compassionate Redeemer of sinners, let my soul adore Thee, let all my life be spent in Thy service, let all my inward parts yearn after Thee. My poor soul desires, O Lord, desires to think of Thee, to scan Thy wonders, and to know to the full how good Thou art to sinners, lest, falling into despair on account of my sins, I should by deliberate choice estrange myself from Thy goodness; but that, so fixing my mind on Thee, and believing in Thee, Who art the Truth, I may now at last desist from my evil ways, and reset for the doing what is right a will that has been warped and bent by sins and wicked deeds.

I know, O Lord, that Thou hast made out of nothing all things that are; that they were not, and Thou madest them; but Thou Who madest them hast ever been, and time was never when Thou wast not. Thou wast ever good, ever omnipotent; and therefore whatever things Thou hast made, Thou hast made them good. Thou, therefore, Who hast been, art, and wilt be, ever; and Who earnest not out of non-existence into being; as Being has been ever Thine, so have also goodness and omnipotence been ever Thine. And hence Thou hast no other law of being than goodness and omnipotence; and what is to Thee the law of being is by that very fact goodness and omnipotence; and so Thou canst not be other than good and omnipotent. And so of all that may in like manner be predicated or believed of Thee.

Yes, Thou truly art, and there is nothing else besides Thee, and Thou in Thyself simply art. For what Thou art now Thou dost not anon cease to be, but what Thou art now that Thou art ever. But the creature's essence, whose being has not always been, but which has through Thee and by Thee come from non-existence into existence, is not identically the same as goodness and omnipotence; but when it is good, and when it has the capacity of doing good, the character and the capacity are alike from Thee, Thee Who art essentially good and omnipotent. Thou madest every creature good; and yet Thou hast not given to every creature, good though it have been made by Thee, reason by which to understand Thee. And although every creature praise Thee, and proclaim Thee its Creator and its Governor, yet every creature doth not understand Thee, but only the rational creation and that which Thou hast made to Thine image and likeness.

[§ 95.] IV. The praise of the Creator by the whole creation. And yet that creation even which Thou hast not gifted with intelligence praises Thee, when the rational creation beholds that it has been by Thee created so good, and ordered on so exquisite a plan. And this is being praised by it; Thy being understood, namely, by the rational creation to have made it good and ordered it exquisitely. But Thou hast distinguished between man's nature and that nature which is not gifted with intelligence; Thou hast distinguished by ordaining that human nature [i.e. humanity], on whose account Thou madest that other [i.e. the irrational] creation, should dispose it according to Thy will, and should exact and receive from it, by Thy allowance, the means of its own sustentation.

But man--for he is composed of two parts different in origin from each other, soul, namely, and body--receives the aliment needful for his bodily life from the creature, but draws the sup plies of his spiritual life from the Creator; and yet both one and the other from the Creator. Man, in short, here in this transitory state lives the life of the flesh so long as he is nourished with human food, and lives the life of the soul so long as he observes the will and keeps the commandments of his Creator. And just as he dies the death of the flesh if he is not supported by human food, so does he die the death of the soul when he disobeys the Divine commands. Man therefore, compound that he is of soul and flesh, lives in his flesh and in his soul by doing what God bids, for by such a course he merits a blissful life with his Creator in the life eternal. But if he essay to deviate from the course enjoined by his Creator, and seek in preference to live according to the desires of the flesh--which indeed is not truly to live, but rather a miserable forfeiting of life--it must clearly appear to the attentive thinker, that in man thus degraded is not the fashion of that perfect Man who was created to the image of God, but rather a resemblance to the brute whose behaviour he takes care to copy. And in such an event may it truly enough be averred that he is dead, doomed, as he is, to eternal death should he persist in this course to the end.

[§ 96.] V. The resemblance of man to his Creator. Now God the Creator made man to His Image and Likeness, for He made him a rational being. And just as God is good in will, so is man, made after His likeness, good also in will; in this respect like the Creator, the Creator good in will, man good in will; but in another respect unlike Him, for the Creator is eternally good by and of Himself, and good by the law of His Being, whereas man is only good as imitating Him who eternally and essentially is of and by Himself good. The Creator, as I have just said, is good in will; man, made to the image of the Creator, is good in will, but with a difference, thus: The Creator neither wills to be nor can be other than good, whether in being or in will: for will and can, will and power are His to be, His essence; whereas in man will and power are separable and separate from being. If, however, man conforms with the will of God, and wills what God does, he exhibits in himself the Image of God; and if he persevere in this even to the end, he merits, by the operation of the Divine compassion, to be close joined through eternity to his Creator's will, and never again to be capable of detachment from it any more for ever. And just as in the Creator, Being is not separable from will, or will separable from Being, so too, after his measure, in man, once entered on that happy state of existence, shall will be, by his Creator's gift, as unchangeable in him as being; the which being shall be as undoubtedly able to do whatever it may will as from subsisting in an undoubtedly happy state it shall be an undoubtedly happy being. And then shall man have free power of choice, truly free because set free entirely from all evil: according as here in this transitory state he wills, so long as he lives, to do, God's grace working in him, what God commands, and to leave undone what God forbids.

[§ 97.] VI. Man is composed of two parts; by the one of which he is raised to highest things, and by the other dragged down to lowest. Now man is composed of two parts; one of them in the order of soul, the other in the order of flesh. The soul's natural tendency--for the soul is a spiritual substance--is by the very law of its being to objects above itself; but that of the flesh--since the flesh passes forth from desire into the region of carnal appetites--is by a sort of inherent law towards things below. Between these two natural components of man stands the will, occupying as it were a middle place, and gifted with free power of choice. And should the will, by an exercise of this free choice, yoke and conjoin itself with the soul, which by an inherent law tends upwards, then soul and will by their united strength--not, however, without inspiration from Divine grace--raise the flesh upwards with themselves to a highest sphere, and lodge it there, to live without end in eternal happiness--happiness, indeed; for now at last there is no repugnancy henceforward between flesh and soul, but they have evermore one only love, one only will; and then shall the will of God the Creator and man the creature whom He made to His own image and likeness, be simply, absolutely one; for God shall be all in all

(1 Cor. xv. 28). But if, on the contrary, the will, by means of that same free choice, yokes itself with the desires of the flesh, which by a certain inherent tendency incline to lowest things, then the will, making so ill a use of its free choice, and with it the flesh unite in dragging downwards the soul, bereft of assistance from above; and the sins of man plunge the whole man, man's self--his soul, namely, and his body--into destruction, so as henceforth to possess nothing but ill, and endure nothing but torment.

[§ 98.] VII. Here man prays God not to allow him to make ill use of his free power of choice. O my sweetest Lord and most merciful God, my Creator, my Salvation, my Life, my Hope, my Consolation, and my Refuge, do Thou govern and uphold my power of free choice by Thy grace and by Thy all-merciful loving-kindness, that I may not by an ill use of it offend Thee, my dearest Creator; and whensoever evil charms me, or ever I carry it out in act, crush and destroy all my evil desire. Rather would I, O dearest Father, be dragged even against my will by Thee, and thrown manacled and fettered into some neglected corner of Thy house, and left lying there, than that I should be severed from Thee; and there, though I may not, through my sins, be allowed to gaze on Thy all-merciful Face, yet be it mine at least to listen to the gladness and the joy of them that wait on Thee.

Who, sweetest Creator of mankind, who can measure that unspeakable goodness of Thine, where with Thou hast loved our human nature to such excess of love, as not only to have created it when it was not, but for love of it to have become Thyself a creature? Who can have heart so hard, so stony hard, as, knowing and scanning well Thy so great love to man whom Thou createdst, not to be softened, and melted through and through into acknowledgment and adoration of Thy sweetness? Yes, yes, my soul; yes, yes, my heart, and all you inward parts of me; the wonder is that you ever can forget the so great charity and the so great mercy of your Creator. See, see, poor man, what thy Creator and what thy Lord has done. He whose TO BE ever is and ever was, He the Un changeable and the Invisible, He the Incomprehensible and the Immeasurable, He after a wondrous and ineffable manner, without setting aside or foregoing His own TO BE, debased Himself' (Phil. ii. 7) in thy behalf, when in thy behalf He willed to be made a creature, that so He might reconcile thee, who earnest out of non-existence into being, to Himself, who, so far from coming into being out of non-existence, had Being everlastingly; reconcile thee by so intimate a fellowship; and reconciling, remodel and restore thee to thy pristine dignity; and lead thee thus reformed home to His own TO BE. Lo now, my God and my Creator, lo now Thou seest where I have landed in my meditations; and withal Thou seest how thus musing my poor soul is even yet enslaved to vanities and follies; for if, pitifully regarded by Thy grace, I begin at any time to meditate as may seem to tend to some little my soul's profit, my mind, so unstable is it, so almost void of all good, soon, soon, too soon glides away into vanity and harm; unstable and empty as the chaff which the veriest breath of wind blows from the threshing-floor.

Therefore, seeing, as Thou dost, that my mind is so inconstant, so sluggish, and so indolent in meditating on what is serviceable, so eager and so zealous to what is harmful, bethink Thee not of my sinfulness. I am a sinner; I confess it, I confess it; I am a graceless sinner, an unclean sinner; and yet I do not leave Thee, dearest Jesus Christ. Wilt Thou or wilt Thou not, I will not let Thee go, weak though the hand be that detains Thee: Thou shalt go from me not except Thou absolve me from every thought of sin. Strike me, correct me, chide me; ay, chastise Thy servant; and chastise him, until by Thy unspeakable goodness Thou lead me to the glory of Thy vision face to face.

TWENTIETH MEDITATION

[§ 99.] Complaint of the soul banished from God. My sinful soul is not content, O Lord, is not content with trusting that its sins are removed out of the abundance of Thy unspeakable mercy; it would fain have the grief removed which it suffers from the withholding of Thy Countenance, by at least giving vent to its complaint in Thy Presence. For it is absent from Thee, its Lord, and that on account of its iniquities.

I begin my meditation, then, by proposing that my sorrow be consoled; and, lo, the very gaining of the comfort is a fresh aggravation of the sorrow. For the very quest after consolation awakens in my mind a fresh consciousness of sorrow. I should not seek for consolation were I not conscious of my grief; for the search after the soothing repose of consolation is prompted by the consciousness of grief; and yet that very search does but quicken and enhance the consciousness. And thus the oftener the picture of my grief is set before the mind, the more vividly is it aggravated and increased. What, then, am I doing? Is it really so that the exhibition of one's grief ever yields by way of return some solace, however little?

Let me unfold, O Lord, before the eye of Thy mercy the bitternesses of my soul, all the bitternesses that spring from its accumulated iniquities, and hedge it round about; for, but for those iniquities, it would not have to endure, as it does, its estrangement from Thy all-lovely Face. 'Tis hence that comes the utmost of my grief, O Lord; the know ledge that Thy clemency has been so grievously offended by my iniquity, and that by that very iniquity my heart's eye is blinded so that it cannot see the light of Thy desirable splendours. Thou madest me to rejoice in Thee; but I have made myself so base that I blush to appear in Thy Presence. For my iniquities are gone over my head, and as a heavy burden are become heavy upon me' (Ps. xxxvii. 5): my mind is bewildered with the stupefying gall of wickedness; my soul is stained with vices and uncleanness; my heart is filled with the corruption of injustice; my soul is ensnared in sinful toils, and all my whole being burdened with a mountain of crimes. Who, then, will succour me, plunged as I am in such a deep of miseries? Who will stretch out a hand to help me? What! have I, and I alone--alas, 'tis too true--exasperated my God so grievously, that neither He nor any of His creatures needs notice me any more? Woe is me! Why, why did I stay in the world even for an hour after I was born, that I should do so great injury against my God? Why is life so long allowed me that I should only squander it in vicious affections?

And yet why do I deplore the lengthening out of life, when I see that that very lengthening is God's invitation to me to repent? Knowest thou not,' says the Apostle, that the benignity of God leadeth thee to penance?' But according to thy hardness and impenitent heart, thou treasurest up to thyself wrath against the day of wrath, and revelation of the just judgment of God' (Rom. ii. 4, 5). Life, in short, is allowed me that I may amend it. And why, then, is it not amended? And if life is prolonged for penance, why is that penance so in sincere? If God has mercy on my soul, standing aloof for a little space, why, why has it not mercy on itself by setting aside its sins? O senseless hardness of this heart of mine! Death is delayed, that life may be reformed; and yet, as life is lengthened out, a death more dire is laid up in store for me. Trouble, trouble either way. While I am in the body, I am absent from the Lord (2 Cor. v. 6); and I dread the while, lest for my sins it should be worse with me out of the body, to leave the body. I grieve that I am defrauded of God's Presence; and I dread to encounter a removal from this body of corruption, although no otherwise can I be inducted to that Presence.

What is it, what is it, O Lord, that this poor sinner's heart beholds, and yet knows not how to syllable? Indeed, O good Jesus, to be dissolved and to be with Thee is by far the very best of is sues. Why, then, is not that desired which is surely known to be the best? To be dissolved and to be with Christ (Phil. i. 23) is bliss; to be pinioned with the body and kept away from Christ is misery. Why, then, fear to be rid of the misery, and not desire to possess the bliss? No; this, this is the reason why we do not desire to be dissolved from the body, this is it; that we are doubtful whether, after the dissolution, it will be granted unto us to be with Christ.

[§ 100. The soul's absence from God.] And thus it comes about that our lodging in the flesh is judged a profitable thing; for so long as we live in it, amendment of life is looked forward to with hope. O the sins of men! For by their merit human life, misery that it is, is yet accounted profitable. Is it not so, that all this present life is misery? And this misery, albeit it is profitable in some instances even to the just, that they may augment their merit, proves to be the last of all necessities for the wicked, that they may provide themselves the medicine of penance. But note the difference; this one and the self-same misery challenges the grief of good minds, whilst by the unwise it is all too dangerously loved. For persisting in love of it, they move from this very misery on to misery everlasting; and their passage through a course of misery on to misery is effected in miserable sort: since this present misery is spent in the labour that their lusts impose, and the misery that is to be immediately after, and that shall never end, is endured in never-ending sorrow. Nay, indeed, that same misery will be all the sharper punishment as this life's misery shall have been lengthened with a view to repentance. O Father, Thou who truly ART, since Thou in highest sense art--for Thou art always the Self-same, and Thy years shall not fail' (Ps. ci. 28)--come and succour one oppressed with misery. For if the misery which, by the disposition of Thy mercy, I endure for the avoiding of a greater misery--and avoided it may be by the pursuit of penance--be protracted, why yet is this misery so much loved? Why do I love what I must needs forego so soon, and not desire what might secure beatitude when the misery of this present life is ended? If I am not able to love, as it were well that I should, the bliss which Thou dost promise to those that love Thee, why do I not at any rate dread the punishments Thou threatenest to them that despise Thee, one of whom--O grief--I am? For if I dreaded them, surely I should amend my ways, in some degree at least; and so would it be brought to pass that, through Thy mercy's gift, I should attain sometime to the goal of love by the way of fear and chastisement.

But why do I not fear Thy judgments, unless it be. that I am so remiss in meditating on them? And, lest I should be able to think about them as frequently as I ought, my faults stand ever in my way, flattering and cajoling me with pleasures and allurements fraught with death. O Lord, O Lord, behold, I am Thy servant, and the son of Thy handmaid' (Ps. cxv. 16); for, although a sinner, yet the son of Thy holy Church. But what have I said! How could I dare to use the words, Thy servant,' when I know full well that I am the servant of sins? for whosoever committeth sin is the servant of sin' (St. John viii. 34); and I fail not to sin incessantly; I am the servant, then, of sin; how, then, could I dare to say Thy servant'? No, no; I would not have said the word, were it not that, presuming on Thy unspeakable compassion, I could even dare to say it; for servant though I be of sin by the infirmity I am enduring, yet I am Thy servant by the desire which, I rejoice to know, has been granted me by Thy adorable goodness. I am, then, Thy ser-

vant, O Lord; if not in act and habit, yet at least in affection and will.
But herein am I in wretched and most deplorable plight; that, though I
own myself Thy servant, yet I do not strive to render Thee the honour
due unto my Lord, as it were well I should. For if I did, nothing, nothing could ever allure me from the thought of Thee, and from the desire
of understanding Thee, or from the blissful sweetness of Thy love. O
my Lord, O my Lord, why, since Thou art my Lord, do I not live as
servant of Thine ought to live? I own Thee for my God, and I desire to
be Thy servant; why fail I, then, in practice to lead a life worthy of
Thy servant?

[**§ 101. Complaint of the soul banished from God.**] But
why should I not seek for the cause of this very misery, since I cannot
doubt that it has been merited by my iniquity? Ah me! Why do I live?
Why do I live so long, who live so ill? To live is granted me that death
may be avoided; and that very living is found to be even worse than
death. O, all-wise Maker of mankind and me, Thou givest me opportunity of endeavouring to prepare for the contemplation of Thy beauty;
and I fail not day by day to show myself vile and viler still. What, O
my God, more lovely than Thy unspeakable glory? and what more vile
than my iniquity? O deepest heart of mine, feast thee upon sighs; so
making sorrow thy pursuit shalt thou be illuminated with fresh beauty,
and thine inward eye the easier lifted to behold the glory of the Light
Supreme. O inmost soul of mine, away now with all thy foolish flights,
set thyself to gaze only on the Divine Effulgence, and for desire of It
shed plentiful showers of tears; so shall thy countless filthy stains be
washed out by their flooding tide, and the pristine beauty lavished on
thee by the bountiful Framer of all things be restored to thee again, by
the providence of His mercy. And you, O my inward parts, strain all
your powers, ply all your best endeavours, in quest of that pure, that
simple, that eternal, that sole blessed Good, Whose light shall banish
all your gloom, Whose limpid flood shall wash out all your stains,
Whose freedom shall loosen all the bonds that bind you down enslaved
to vice, Whose strength shall inform all your weakness, Whose wisdom chase away your folly, Whose life save you from eternal death,
and make you sharers of His immortality. O Good surpassing all
goods--for from Thee and in Thee all goods are, forasmuch as all
goods art Thou--I confess that my ills are all too great, for too many
and grievous are my sins, and my faults increased past measurement;
for hitherto my mind has--O how miserably!--been intently set upon
them. O ills of mine, why have you so cruelly overridden me, and es-

tranged me from the All-Good? O sins of mine, why hold you me so mercilessly entangled in your meshes, and suffer me not to enter into holy freedom? O faults of mine, why do you make my heart cling to you,--just as the anteater's tongue [12] is wont to enthrall insects by its own sheer tenacity,--and allow me not to escape from you? Be troubled, O my mind; faint, faint, my heart; shrink with horror, O my soul; and you, my eyes, grow dim with weeping. For what is to be found more wretched every way than I am? All things ever keep inviolate their appointed order; but as to mine, I violate it daily.

[§ 102. The soul's return to God.] But He who bears so long with the sinner, will He refuse to receive the penitent? I will go therefore to my Father, though I be a worthless child; I will go to Him, the innocence He gave me squandered all; I will go, famished with long, long hunger that I endure unfed with His heavenly converse; I. will go, and I will say to Him,' Father, I am not now worthy to be called Thy SON' (St. Luke xv. 19); I do not venture to strive with Thy children for place of dignity; I only ask for mercy among Thy servants; make me,' therefore, as one of Thy hired servants.' Thus, merciful Father, shall Thy compassion be told abroad; and Thy riches will be none the less if Thou run to meet me as I desire to return to Thee, and if Thou fold me in the arms of Thy mercy, and bid me be adorned with the ring of faith and the robe of justice, and deign to say of me to Thy angels, This My son was dead, and is come to life again; he was lost, and is found' (ib. 24). But who, O all-good and admirable Father, shall give me to eat with worthy sentiments of faith and holiness of that fatted calf, given by Thee and immolated for my redemption on the altar of the Cross? For who is that mystic Calf, so meek in the death of sacrifice, so health-giving when partaken of as food; who but that Thine own only-begotten Son, whom Thou didst not spare but didst deliver up for us all? (Rom. viii. 32.) 'Tis He, O Lord, 'tis He with whose sweetness my heart pants to be refreshed; and this is He whom my mind longs to love before all things. 'Tis He by whose absence from her my soul complains with many sighs that she should be so estranged from Him. But if I desire the Son do I in this neglect the Father? Far be it from me. Nay, how can it be possible? For the Father who begot is not other (by nature) than the Son who was begotten; and again, what the Son is that the Father is, albeit the Father is not the same Person with the' Son. And how can I desire the Father and the Son, that Love of Father and of Son removed, who is not other (by nature) than what Father and Son is, and yet is another Person than Father and than Son? No, it cannot be.

Say therefore, O my soul, to thy Maker, to Father, Son, and
Holy Ghost, one God, I have sought Thy Face; Thy Face, O Lord, will
I seek out' (Ps. xxvi. 8). See, O Lord; see, I seek, I ask, I knock; when
am I to find, when am I to have, when is the door to open to me? To
Thee, O Lord, lie open all the secrets of my heart. Thou seest that the
Presence of Thy Face is my sole hope of consolation. Ah me! How far
am I, what a distant outcast am I, from that unspeakable joy that His
Presence gives! How, then, shall I be comforted? How indeed, unless
the beauty of that Thy Face beam upon me, whereon hangs all my
hope of consolation? So then, O my God, let my eyes fail for Thy
word, saying, When wilt Thou comfort me? (Ps. cxviii. 82.) Have regard, then, O my God, to the one only desire of my soul; have regard
to the sigh of my heart, and set my tears in Thy sight' (Ps. lv. 9), tears
which I shed for very grief, while my soul faints from the withholding
of Thy Face; for my life is wasted with grief, and my years in sighs'
(Ps. xxx. 11).

Have mercy on me, O Lord, have mercy on me. In season,
out of season, will I cry to Thee, and never let Thee rest until Thou
gladden me with the Presence of Thy Face; and refuse myself all comfort; and punish myself with simply mourning over the absence of Thy
Face. O Face of God, all glory! O Countenance, all light! So long as I
see Thee not, so long shall my soul re main in gloom. But how long, O
cruel bitter absence of God's Face, how long wilt thou torture me? O
wearisome life in this vain world, how long wilt thou hold shut up as it
were in prison, bound by the bonds of thy vanities, my soul, so woful
by its dwelling here in thee? O my soul, what is it that charms thee in
this mortal life? Why dost thou not speed thee to the blissful vision of
God, whence thou art held aloof by the merit of thy fault? Why dost
thou not loathe this exile from the Face of God, and thy enthralment in
the chains of this garish life? Why dost thou not yearn with utmost
desire to have share in the joys of that blissful life, and be far away
from the filth of this grovelling existence? Why dost thou not fly from
the one, and hie thee to the other? If this life is given thee as a breathing time, with peace in possibility, why dost thou dally? Why not offer
God such penance as that He may for give thee thy sins, and in mercy
take thee to Himself? Ay, let my turning be to Thee that Thy mercy
regard me kindly, and Thy compassion confirm me in my longing for
Thy Face, and give me the gift of perseverance; for I believe that I
shall not be severed from Thy bliss if only I grow not weary in my

desires after Thee. Let my soul ever yearn for the glory of Thy Face; my mind love it; my thoughts be intent upon it; my whole heart's affection sigh after it; my tongue speak of it; my whole being be held in thrall with love of it. Only let Thy mercy, while I carry about this mortal body, and wear the fardels of my pilgrim age, bid me be established in Thy fear, enlarged in Thy love, taught in Thy law, devout in Thy precepts, and filled with fires of longing for Thy promises; that, treading vices under foot, and practising all virtues, I may, adorned with these, both please Thee evermore, and soon, soon attain to reach Thee in Thy heaven of bliss, where is given to Thee unending praise, unbounded glory, and honour through eternity. Amen.

[12] [The Benedictines read, sicut gliris hastulam suam tenacitate infectam vincere solet.' Migne's bastulam,' probably a misprint, is hopeless. I propose, as an emendation, sicut gliris hastula suâ tenacitate insecta vincere solet.' If this be the right reading, the corruption is easy to trace. Sicut gliris hastula sua tenacitate insecta vincere solet;' thence sicut gliris hastulam suam tenacitate infectam vincere solet.' The glires of science are a very varied collection of animals, and are said to comprise nearly a third part of the mammalia; but the anteater is the only one of the glires which seems to correspond with the description in the text. Its tongue could scarcely be described better than as a hastula tenacitate suâ vincens;' for, it is an offensive weapon covered with a secretion which is simply irresistible by insects, such is its tenacity. That hastula' not glis' is the subject of the clause lends probability to the emendation; for, since making the correction, I have learnt that, when employed in catching insects, the natural weapon of the anteater coils and twists about as if it possessed a separate vitality of its own;' its shape is that of a large red earthworm, hence a certain suitability in the word hastula." I am inclined to think that the passage is, after all, an interpolation; that, inserted by a strange hand in the margin of a MS., it was introduced into the text of the work by a copyist, who, not familiar with the character, read hastula, sua and insecta for hastula, sua and insecta. The passage thus corrupted, insectam' would soon become infectam.' TR.]

TWENTY-FIRST MEDITATION

[§ 103. THE SOUL OF MAN URGED TO SEEK AND TO FIND ITS GOD. THE MIND AROUSED TO THE CONTEMPLATION OF GOD.]

AND now, poor mortal, avoid for a little while earthly employments, hide thee for a time from thy conflicting thoughts, throw aside thy burden some cares, and postpone to another time all wearisome distractions. Retire for a little space in God, and rest thee for a while in Him. Enter into the closet of thy heart; shut out all except God, and what may help thee in thy quest of Him, and with closed door seek Him. And then say, O my whole heart, say at once to God, I seek Thy Face; Thy Face, O Lord, will I still seek.'

Now, therefore, O Lord my God, teach Thou my heart where and how to seek Thee; when and how to find Thee. If Thou art not here, O Lord, whither shall I go to seek Thee? But if Thou art everywhere, why do I not see Thee here? No; for in truth Thou inhabitest the inapproachable light. But where is the inapproachable light? Or how shall I approach the inapproachable? Or who will lead me into it, that I may see Thee in it? And then, what are the tokens by which I am to seek Thee, what the aspect by which I am to know Thee? O Lord my God, I have never seen Thee, and, I know not what Thou art like.

O what, most high God, what is this far-off exile of Thine to do? What is Thy servant to do, anxious from love of Thee, and far banished from Thy Presence? He yearns to behold Thee, and Thy Face is too far off from him; he longs to approach Thee, and Thy dwelling-place is inapproachable; he desires to find Thee, but knows not the place of Thy rest; and strives to seek Thee, but cannot tell what Thy Face is like.

O Lord, Thou art my God and my Lord, and I have never seen Thee. Thou hast made and re-made me, and all the blessings that I have are of Thy giving; and as yet I do not know Thee. I was created to behold Thee, and as yet I have not attained to the object of my creation. O sad estate of man! for man has foregone that for which he was created. O hard, O cruel lot! What, alas, did he lose, and what did he find? What went, and what remained? He lost the beatitude for which he was created, and he found the misery for which he was never made; that went without which no happiness is, and that remained which of itself is merest misery. And then he ate the bread of sorrows, and knew it not.

Ah, the general anguish of mankind, the universal wailing of the sons of Adam! Our first father had bread to the full, and we cry out for hunger. He abounded, and we are beggars: he so happy in having, so sad in foregoing; we so unhappy in our need, so miserable in our craving! And yet we remain empty. Why did he not keep and guard, when he might have done it so easily, what we lack so grievously? Why, why did he so block out the light, and cover us up in darkness? Why did he filch away our life, and bring in death instead? O woe-begone we! whence are we banished, whither are we driven? Whence hurled headlong, whither fallen low? From our home, to exile; from God and the vision of God, to self and its blindness; from the joys of immortality, to the horror and the bitterness of death. Miserable change! From how great good to how great ill!

Sad loss, sad grief, sad everything! But wo is me, poor me, one of other the poor sons of Eve banished from their God. What have I endeavoured, what achieved? Whither did I tend, and what have I reached? To what did I aspire, and where am I now sighing, I sought for peace, and there is no good; and for the time of healing, and behold trouble'? (Jer. xiv. 19.)

I reached forth to God, and I stumbled on self. I sought rest in my secret place, and I met with trouble and sorrow' (Ps. civ. 3) in my inmost parts. I wished to return in the joy of my soul, and lo, I am forced to roar with the groaning of my heart' (Ps. xxxvii. 9). Happiness was the goal of my hope, and lo, sigh is crowded upon sigh. And Thou, O Lord, how long? How long, O Lord, wilt Thou forget me unto the end? how long dost Thou turn away Thy Face from me?' (Ps. xii. 1.) When wilt Thou look on me and hear me? When wilt Thou lighten mine eyes and show me Thy Face? When wilt Thou restore Thyself to me?

Look on me, O Lord, and hear me, and en lighten me, and show me Thyself. Restore Thyself to me, that it may be well with me; Thou, without whom it goes so ill with me. Direct, O Lord, my labours and my endeavours unto Thee, for without Thee I am nothing worth. Thou invitest me; help me, O Lord, I pray Thee, that I sigh not from despair, but breathe again and hope. Lord, I pray Thee, for it is soured by its lonesomeness, sweeten my heart with Thy consolations. () Lord, I pray Thee, for I have begun to seek Thee hungering, let me not go away empty; I have drawn near famished with want, let me not depart unsatisfied. I have come, a beggar to the Rich, a wretch to the All-merciful; let me not turn back despised and without an alms. And even if I sigh before I can eat, give me something to eat after I have sighed.

O Lord, I am bowed down low, and cannot look up; raise me, that I may lift mine eyes on high. My iniquities are gone over my head' (Ps. xxxvii. 5) and overwhelm me, and as a heavy burden' they press me sore. Rescue me, unburden me; let not the pit shut her mouth upon me' (Ps. lxviii. 16). Be it mine to see Thy light from afar, even from the depth. Teach me to seek Thee; and when I seek, show Thyself; for I can neither seek Thee unless Thou teach me, nor find Thee unless Thou show Thyself to me. Let me seek Thee by desiring, and desire Thee in seeking; let me find Thee by loving, and love Thee in finding. I confess to Thee, O Lord, and I give Thee thanks that Thou hast created me in Thine image, so as ever mindfully to muse on Thee and love Thee. But the image is so defaced by the wear and waste of evil habits, and so befouled with the smoke and stain of sins, that it cannot do that for which it was created unless Thou remake and readorn it. I do not essay to sound Thy depths, O Lord, for I no way match my understanding to such an effort; but I do long in some sort to understand that truth of Thine which my heart believes and loves; for I seek not to understand that I may believe, but I believe that I may understand.

[§ 104. The inapproachable dwelling-place of God.]
Truly, O Lord, this light in which Thou dwellest is an inapproachable light. For in truth there is nothing that can pierce it, so as to see Thee in its midst. And truly, too, I see it not, for it is too bright to be seen: and yet whatever I see, I see by it; like the weak eye which, whatever it beholds, beholds by the sun's light, a light which it is unable to look upon in the sun itself. My understanding cannot aspire to reach it, for it is too bright, therefore it endures it not; nor can the eye of my soul bear to fix too long a gaze upon it, but is stricken by its brightness, quelled by its fulness, overwhelmed by its immensity, bewildered by its grandeur. O supreme and inapproachable Light, holy and blessed Truth, who art far from me, near though I be to Thee, how far removed art Thou from my ken, present though I be to Thy sight! Thou art alto-

gether present every where, and I do not see Thee; I move in Thee and am in Thee, and I cannot approach Thee; Thou art within me and round about me, and I feel Thee not.

Thus ever dost Thou in Thy light and Thy bliss hide Thyself from my soul; and she lingers on in her gloom and sadness. She strains her eye, and descries not Thy beauty; she listens, but catches not Thy harmony; she longs for Thee, but Thy fragrance breathes not on her; she feels for Thee, but nothing of Thee answers to her touch; she tastes, and discerns not Thy sweetness. For Thou hast all these in Thyself, beauty, harmony, fragrance, grace, and sweetness, after Thine own ineffable manner, since Thou hast bestowed them on created things in their own manner, as we recognise after a sensible manner; but the senses of my soul are dulled, stupefied, and blunted by the old disease of sin. What art Thou, O Lord; what art Thou? Truly Thou art Life, and Truth, and Goodness, and Bliss, and Eternity, and every good!

[§ 105. The goodness of God, the creative Life.] Rouse thyself now, O my soul; exert all thy powers, and think what that good is; how great and of what degree it is. For if all good things taken severally are delectable, think, O think, how delectable must be that good which includes all goods and the delightsomeness of all; a delightsomeness, not such as we have by experience known in created things, but as different from that as the Creator transcends the creature. For if created life be good, how good is the Life creative! If achieved salvation be a joyous thing, how joyous must that Salvation be by, which all salvation was achieved! If wisdom in the observation of visible things be a worthy object of love, how loveable must that Wisdom be which created all things out of nothing! In short, if in all delectable things there are many and great delights, what and how great must be the delightsomeness of Him who created all delightsome things!

And he who shall enjoy this good, what shall he have I rather, what shall he not have? What ever he shall wish, he will have; and not wish, he shall not have. Ay, he shall have blessings of body and of soul such as ear hath not heard, eye hath not seen, and heart of man hath not conceived.

Why, then, dost thou wander wide, poor child of earth, in thy search after goods for body and soul? Love the One Good, in whom all good things are, and it is enough. For what, O my flesh, dost thou love? What dost Thou desire, O my soul? Whatever you love, whatever you desire, it is there. If beauty delights you, fulgebunt justi sicut sol' (St. Matt. xiii. 43)--the just shall shine as the sun. Or if fleetness, or strength, or suppleness of body, such as nothing may resist; erunt similes angelis Dei' (St. Luke xx. 36)--they shall be like the angels of God, for it is sown a natural body, it shall rise a spiritual body;' spiritual, that is to say, in capacity, though not in essence. If health and long life have charms for you, healthful eternity and eternal health are there, for the just shall live for evermore' (Wisdom v. 16), and the salvation of the just is from the Lord' (Ps. xxxvi. 39). If abundance, they shall be satisfied when the glory of God shall appear' (Ps. xvi. 15). If melody, there the angels sing together without end to God. If satisfaction, they shall be inebriated with the plenty of Thy house' (Ps. xxxv. 9). If aught and every pure and stainless pleasure have attraction for you, Thou shalt make them drink of the torrent of Thy pleasure' (Ps. xxxv. 9). If wisdom, the Wisdom of God shall Himself display Himself to them eternally. If friendship, they shall love God more than themselves, and God will love them more than they love themselves; for they shall love Him, and in Him, one another; and He will love Himself, and them in Himself. If concord, all of them will have one will; for they shall have no will but God's only. If power, they shall have perfect mastery of their own will, as God has of His. For, as God's will shall be the exact measure of His power, so in Him shall their power be as their will. For, as they shall will nothing apart from Him, even so shall He will whatever they shall will, and what He shall will cannot by any possibility but be. If honour and riches, God will set His good and faithful servants over many things; yea, they shall be called the sons of God, and gods; and where the Son is, there shall they be also, heirs indeed of God, and joint-heirs with Christ' (Rom. viii. 17). If true security, they will assuredly be sure that they shall not lose their treasure by any choice of theirs, and that their lover Lord will not take it from His lovers; and that there is nothing stronger than God, that it should sever an unwilling God and His unwilling creatures from each other.

But what and how great is the joy there, where such and so great is the good! O heart of man, poor heart; heart worn with woes, ay, over whelmed with woes; what, what would be thy joy if thou hadst all these blessings, and hadst them in abundance I Ask thine inmost self if it can com pass all its own joy that shall spring from its own so great bliss. Assuredly, if any other soul whom thou didst love even as thyself enjoyed the very same bliss as thou, thy joy would be doubled; for thou wouldst rejoice not one whit less for him than for thyself. And in like manner, if two, or three, or many more had the very same happiness as thyself, thou wouldst rejoice for each several soul among them as thou didst for thyself, if thy love for each of them were equal to thy love of thyself. In that perfect charity, therefore, of innumerable blessed angels and holy souls, in the home where none loves any other less than he loves himself it is alike true that each several soul, each several angel, shall rejoice for the sake of every other one no less than for his own sake.

If, then, the heart of man can scarce compass its own joy, to be begotten of its own so great bliss, how shall it be able to compass so many and so great joys? For 'tis true indeed that as great as is the love of any to another, so great will be his joy in that other's good. But, O, in that perfect bliss, each one will love his God more, incomparably more, than will be his love for himself, and for all other beings with himself; and therefore he will rejoice more, more beyond all power of counting or imagining; he will rejoice more in the happiness of God than in his own happiness and that of all others besides. But and if they so love God with all their heart, with all their mind, with all their soul, that all heart, all mind, all soul shall not be sufficient for His worthiness to be loved, why, then, the just will so rejoice in that supreme felicity with all their heart, all their mind, all their soul, that all heart, all mind, all soul shall not be sufficient for the fulness of their joy.

[§ 106. The fulness of joy.] My God and my Lord, my hope and the joy of my heart, speak Thou to my soul, and tell me if this be the joy of which Thou tellest us by Thy Son, Ask, and you shall receive; that your joy may be full' (St. John xvi. 24). For I have found a joy, full and more than full. For though heart be full, life full, soul full, the whole being full of it, still, still there will be joy remaining and overflowing beyond measure. For not the whole of that joy shall enter into those who enjoy it, but they, wholly rejoicing, shall enter into it.

Speak, O Lord, speak to Thy servant interiorly in his heart, and tell me: is this the joy into which Thy servants are to enter, who shall enter into the joy of their God? Certainly, that joy wherewith Thine elect are to rejoice eye hath not seen, nor ear heard, neither hath it entered into the heart of man' (1. Cor. ii. 9) in this life. And I, O Lord have as yet neither said nor thought how great will be the joy of those Thy blessed ones. Only this can I say or think: they will rejoice even as they love, and they will love even as they know. O how perfectly will they know Thee, O Lord, and how entirely will they love Thee! No, in this life of a truth eye hath not seen, nor ear heard, neither hath it entered into the heart of man, how in that life Thy saints shall know Thee, and shall Thee. I pray Thee, O my God, grant me to know Thee, to love Thee, to rejoice in Thee; and if cannot in this life do so to the full, at least let me advance day by day more and more, until at last that to the full' shall be mine. Here let the knowledge of Thee increase in me, that maybe full; here let Thy love grow in me, that there it may be full; that thus my joy here may be great, great in hope; so as there to be full, full in Thee.

O Lord, Thou by Thy Son commandest, rather, Thou dost counsel us to seek, and Thou dost promise that we shall receive, that our joy may be full. Be it so, O Lord; I ask what Thou dost counsel by Thy Wonderful, Thy Counsellor, so as to receive what Thou dost promise by Thy Truth; that so my joy may be full. And meanwhile let my mind draw from thence its musings, and my tongue eloquence; let my heart love it, and my mouth speak of it; let my soul hunger after it, and my flesh thirst for it, and my whole being desire it, until at last I enter into the joy of my Lord, who is Three and One, blessed for ever and ever. Amen.

THE END.

INDEXES

Index of Scripture References

Genesis [1]1:26[2]37:27[3]45:26

Exodus [4]3:14

Judges [5]16:14

1 Kings [6]2:3

2 Kings [7]12:23

2 Chronicles [8]6:30

Job [9]3:16[10]3:23[11]10:22[12]42:11

Psalms [13]2:10[14]7:3[15]10:7[16]12:1[17]15:11[18]16:8-9
[19]16:15[20]18:6[21]18:13[22]24:6[23]25:4[24]26:1
[25]26:8[26]30:11[27]31:4[28]33:6[29]35:9[30]35:9
[31]36:39[32]37:5[33]37:5[34]37:9[35]37:15[36]39:3
[37]40:5[38]41:4[39]41:5[40]44:3[41]44:3[42]44:13
[43]45:11[44]49:17[45]54:6[46]55:9[47]56:2[48]61:4
[49]65:5[50]68:2[51]68:5[52]68:15[53]68:16[54]73:25
[55]73:25[56]83:3[57]83:3[58]83:10[59]85:17[60]101:28
[61]104:3[62]113:17[63]115:15[64]115:16[65]118:82 [66]126:5[67]135:6

Proverbs [68]3:32[69]8:31[70]10:28

Ecclesiastes [71]1:18[72]7:14[73]9:1

Song of Solomon [74]1:1[75]1:1[76]1:3[77]1:12[78]1:12[79]4:3[80]5:1
[81]5:10[82]5:16

Isaiah [83]5:20[84]9:6[85]9:7[86]12:6[87]14:12[88]14:18-19
[89]26:20[90]40:6[91]53:3[92]53:4[93]53:5[94]53:7
[95]53:9[96]53:12[97]57:1[98]61:7[99]61:10[100]61:10

Galatians [226]3:27

Ephesians [227]5:32

Philippians [228]1:23[229]2:7

Colossians [230]2:3[231]3:1

1 Timothy [232]6:16[233]6:16

2 Timothy [234]2:4[235]2:12

Hebrews [236]1:3[237]5:7

James [238]1:16

Revelation [239]6[240]6:11[241]14:4[242]14:13

Wisdom of Solomon [243]5:16[244]11:25

Sirach [245]2:11[246]24:27[247]38:25[248]47:10

Index of Latin Words and Phrases

Ad hoc enim ipsum paragraphis sunt distinctæ: [249]1

Denique idcirco volui eas ipsas orationes per sententias
paragraphis: [250]1

Duplici stolâ: [251]1

Expectant fideles donec impleatur numerus fratrum suorum ut in die
resurrectionis duplici stolâ, scilicet corporis et animæ perpetuâ
felicitate fruantur.: [252]1

Ferunt odore earum mire solicitari quadrupedes cunctas, sed capitis
torvitate terreri. Quamobrem occultato eo reliqua dulcedine
invitatas corripiunt: [253]1

Formosa Panthera: [254]1

ILLE HOMO: [255]1

Mundâ sindone primæ stolæ spiritum meum involve.: [256]1

Panther dictus, sive quod omnium animalium amicus sit, excepto
dracone; sive quia et sui generis societate gaudet, et ad eandem
similitudinem quicquid accipit reddit. . . . Bestia minutis
orbiculis superpicta, ita ut oculatis ex fulvo circulis nigrâ vel

Also from Benediction Books ...

Wandering Between Two Worlds: Essays on Faith and Art
Anita Mathias
Benediction Books, 2007
152 pages
ISBN: 0955373700

Available from www.amazon.com, www.amazon.co.uk
www.wanderingbetweentwoworlds.com

In these wide-ranging lyrical essays, Anita Mathias writes, in lush, lovely prose, of her naughty Catholic childhood in Jamshedpur, India; her large, eccentric family in Mangalore, a sea-coast town converted by the Portuguese in the sixteenth century; her rebellion and atheism as a teenager in her Himalayan boarding school, run by German missionary nuns, St. Mary's Convent, Nainital; and her abrupt religious conversion after which she entered Mother Teresa's convent in Calcutta as a novice. Later rich, elegant essays explore the dualities of her life as a writer, mother, and Christian in the United States--Domesticity and Art, Writing and Prayer, and the experience of being "an alien and stranger" as an immigrant in America, sensing the need for roots.

About the Author

Anita Mathias was born in India, has a B.A. and M.A. in English from Somerville College, Oxford University and an M.A. in Creative Writing from the Ohio State University. Her essays have been published in The Washington Post, The London Magazine, The Virginia Quarterly Review, Commonweal, Notre Dame Magazine, America, The Christian Century, Religion Online, The Southwest Review, Contemporary Literary Criticism, New Letters, The Journal, and two of HarperSanFrancisco's The Best Spiritual Writing anthologies. Her non-fiction has won fellowships from The National Endowment for the Arts; The Minnesota State Arts Board; The Jerome Foundation, The Vermont Studio Center; The Virginia Centre for the Creative Arts, and the First Prize for the Best General Interest Article from the Catholic Press Association of the United States and Canada. Anita has taught Creative Writing at the College of William and Mary, and now lives and writes in Oxford, England.

9 781849 028028